# NO ONE
## CAN BE AT PEACE
## UNLESS THEY HAVE
# FREEDOM

T0273311

## Other titles by Michael Simanga

*44 on 44: Forty-Four African American Writers on the Election of Barack Obama the 44th President of the United States* (Co-editor)

*In the Shadow of the Son: A Novel*

*Amiri Baraka and the Congress of African People: History and Memory*

*Brilliant Fire! Amiri Baraka: Poems, Plays, Politics for the People* (Co-editor)

# NO ONE
## CAN BE AT PEACE
## UNLESS THEY HAVE
# FREEDOM

ESSAYS • POEMS • THOUGHTS • LESSONS

# MICHAEL SIMANGA

FOREWORD BY
## HAKI R. MADHUBUTI

**Third World Press Foundation**
Chicago

## Third World Press Foundation
Publishers since 1967

thirdworldpressfoundation.com     facebook.com/ThirdWorldPress

Design by Lasana D. Kazembe

Front cover:
Malik Simanga in the Waterfall Room at the National Museum of African
American of African American History and Culture. Photo by Michael Simanga

Back cover:
Photo by Leesa Richards

ISBN: 9780883783740
Library of Congress Control Number: 2017955543

Printed in the United States of America

22 21 20 19 18     7 6 5 4 3 2 1

Publishing Black Writers *Fearlessly* for Fifty Years!
(1967-2017)

"You can't separate peace from freedom because no one can be at peace unless he has his freedom."

**Malcolm X**

for the people
I come from
those before me
those after me
those on the way

mps

# CONTENTS

# Foreword

## Citizenship and Struggle

Dr. Michael Simanga poet, activist, writer and scholar, whose life I have watched and been somewhat involved in over the last fifty years has given to the reading public a book that is an insider's view, as well as a personal memoir of Black Struggle over the last century or so. *No One Can Be at Peace Unless They Have Freedom* is his definitive insight and on-sight witness and participant in the international battle for human rights. This is a chronicle of the many confrontations that he and others have endured in our lifetime. Yet, it is much more than that, for fundamentally, he writes about Black people's commitment toward the eradication of evil and his and other's clear embracing of that which is good, just, right and correct in our multi-century fight for freedom.

He has given us an analytical, intelligent, and emotional call to all people, in particular, Black people to take hold and acknowledge the coming storms and hurricanes that are human made and a hundred times the size of Katrina. He writes that, "history is made by forward motion." This statement can be applied to the life's work of Carter G. Woodson, W.E.B. Du Bois, and Vincent Harding and countless others. His emphasis on Black human rights and citizenship is in keeping with the two recently elected Black mayors, Chokwe Lumumba of Jackson, MS (recently deceased, his son just won his election to the mayorship) and Ras Baraka of Newark, NJ. Their arrival into positions of empowerment is a direct result of their and each mayor's family's deep participation in National and International Struggle.

Like many activist in our tradition, Simanga has been lovingly mentored. His history of street organizing and membership in Black organizations have placed him in the unique position of having an answer:

*we are fighting for our humanity, to be whole, to be who we are in concert with the rest of humanity without the necessity to yield the parts of us that others find offensive because of the narratives created to diminish us and justify our exploitation.*

This book is carefully and strategically wrapped throughout in well-thought out essays, poems, personal thoughts, and lessons for the reader looking for more than top of the head responses like those received from presidents of historically Black colleges and universities who recently with big grins on their faces visited Mr. Trump's White House. This is a critical document that demands that readers think, rethink, and continue to re-access where we are as Black Individuals, families, communities, organizations, institutions, businesses, scholars and of course, artists. There is little bitterness here; rather, this is a loving reminder and refresher course for veterans of Black Struggle and an urgent call and confirmation for the newly initiated. Most certainly, after the deaths of Trayvon Martin, Tamir Rice, Sandra Bland, Laquan McDonald, Philando Castile and countless others—pre- and post-Charlottesville, Virginia, I find this book over-needed.

Simanga is a poet/writer who consciously understands, has been educated within, around, sitting at the knees of Black Elders (his mother and father are two of them), standing at the door of "here I come," fighting and embracing the one undisputed equalizer in a literate culture, language. He has emerged with mind, body, and soul intact and elevated to become one of the few "cultural scientist" of the first order. He is original in his use and exploration of liberated love language. A language that is poetic and musical, reaffirming that our communication—private and public—must be insightful accounts of self-determination at all levels of human activity.

Dr. Simanga was instructed and inspired by the artists, scholars and activists of the Black Arts Movement. He pays tribute in this defining text to Amiri Baraka, Sonia Sanchez, Ron Milner, Muhammad Ali, Marvin Gaye, Maya Angelou, Aneb Kgositsile and others. He pays special attention

to the work of Robert F. Williams and his wife, Mable as well as the revolutionary Haitian Priest, Reverend Gerard Jean-Just. Finally, this book is
the right music to help us drain the swamp of the orange intruder, his fol-
lowers and imitators. Read carefully, take notes, pass on to the young and
not so young as quickly as possible. *No One Can Be at Peace Unless They
Have Freedom* is a "think changer" and should be in all personal and public
libraries.


**Haki R. Madhubuti**
Founder and publisher of Third World Press & Third World Press Foundation and author of *Liberation Narrative: Collected Poems 1966-2009,
Black Men Obsolete: Single and Dangerous*, and *Taking Bullets: Terrorism
and Black Life in Twenty-First Century America*.

# Introduction

## Writing for Change

When I was a child, the voices of Black people sang to me from the pages of Black books and called for me to be a writer. As a practice my writing began in high school in Detroit when the poetry of the Black Arts Movement captured me by speaking from a place and a motion that had previously been unheard but was rocketing forward on fuel from Malcolm X and Black Power.

As a poet, I was writing to be read and performed for Black people and what change we needed—our Black selves armed with unshakable confidence in our movement to be free. From my studies and experience I'd learned that writing is an indispensable tool and weapon for oppressed people fighting for their liberation. Our writers must tell our stories of love and pain, of family and death, ritual and revolt, vision and achievement. In our storytelling and our scholarship our humanity and the aspirations that flow from it is both resistance and revolution. I grew up in and on the Black Arts Movement and write from the voices and pages that sang to me as a child.

The essays, poems, thoughts and observations in this book are pieces written over several years. Some are notes on work that is in progress. Some have been published or performed before. Some have appeared as micro-essays on social media. Most are short pieces that reflect my thinking on a variety of subjects. They are shared here as a contribution to the current discourse for liberation at a time when we need vision, program, organization and action.

It would be impossible to do this work without my family, teachers and comrades, a tribe of artists, activists, workers, scholars, educators and servants of the people.

# Remembrance: A Promise to Our Ancestors

On the coast
of Senegal
watching the waves
singing to the beaches
in hushed tones
and steady rhythms
I stood looking at the water
the endless ocean
extending beyond my sight
the bottomless Atlantic ocean
descending beyond my reach
the powerful ocean
swinging its force
and its centuries of
secrets
back and forth
between continents
spitting debris and empty shells
and the stories of millions
upon the shore
like shells and debris
lying in the sand
waiting to be discovered.

I stood there
searching for the
stories in the sand
and closed my eyes
and smelled the ocean
and the African sun

surrounded my skin
to warm me
because
a chill had fallen
like a misty rain
upon me
causing my bones to
rattle and my
teeth to chatter
and my body to shake
when the voices
of millions of storytellers
began to rise from the sand
and millions more shouted their
tales from the water
in languages I could not decipher
yet completely understood.
The sound of drums
accented with the rattle of
chains and the chatter of
foreign voices and the
shaking of history
knocked me to my knees
demanding my promise
to listen
to witness
to testify
to remember
to live.
My hands
dug deep into the sand
until blood flowed from

underneath my fingernails
and my clothes were
drenched from the spit
of the ocean and clung to my
skin like fungus.

As that promise
passed my lips
(listen)
each word
(witness)
like a breath
(testify)
like a heartbeat
(remember)
like the suckling
of a newborn
(live!)
listen, witness, testify, remember
live
Live!
LIVE!

The words
fell from my mouth
like prayers
skipping across the water
like voices from a choir
chanting, praising, singing
the promise over and over and over.

I stood up on the shore
and the African sun was behind me
and my blood stained the sand
and my shadow fell into the ocean
and the voices were suddenly
quiet
as if hiding
and I felt alone
and exposed
and afraid
as I repeated
my promise
hoping it would
give me courage
and call the voices back
to comfort me and
guide me
and protect me.
I stood there
chanting
praising
singing
when the tide
rolled up around me
and the African sun left me
and the darkness fell upon me
and I was pulled into the ocean
scraping my knees
against a carpet of human bones
the splinters from wooden planks
puncturing my skin
metal tearing at my ankles

and my wrists
while sharks ripped
into my body
leaving a trail of
flesh.

In a moaning
morning silence
I rode the waves
of an ocean
filled with fear
and blood
and shit
and death
until the voices began
to rise again
chanting
praising
singing
in many languages
demanding
that no matter what happens
no matter what happens
I keep my promise
to listen
to witness
to testify
to remember
to live.
My eyes stung
from the salt
of my tears

and my wounds
burned from the salt
of the sea
when the ocean hurled me
upon the shore
of South Carolina
my hands clutching
bones and
pieces of torn
cloth and millions of stories
passed on in the darkness.

With my face buried in the soil
I gasped for fresh air
and vomited bile and blood
between breaths
wrenching the residue of the journey
across the sea
from my body
before
I looked back at the water
searching for the African sun
to warm me again
because
a chill had fallen
like a misty rain
upon me
causing my bones to
rattle and my
teeth to chatter
and my body to shake
when the voices

of millions of storytellers
began to rise from the Southern soil
and millions more shouted their
tales from the water.

the voices began to rise,
and as the languages
melted into each other
there was a
silencing of the drum
and the rattling of
chains grew louder
and the chatter of
unfamiliar foreign voices
became constant
and a violent
shaking of history occurred
as I struggled to my feet
chanting my promise
to listen
to witness
to testify
to remember
to live is a victory
Live for the future
LIVE until our children are born free!

# ONE

NO ONE CAN BE AT PEACE UNLESS THEY HAVE FREEDOM

# 1619 The Good Ship

Cross an ocean
In the belly of Jesus
Restricted motion
In the belly of Jesus

No place to run
In the belly of Jesus
No African sun
In the belly of Jesus

We hear our breath
In the belly of Jesus
We smell our sweat
In the belly of Jesus

We taste our tears
In the belly of Jesus
We wrestle with fear
In the belly of Jesus

Search for light
In the belly of Jesus
We have to fight
In the belly of Jesus

Hide your name
In the belly of Jesus
Cloak our pain
In the belly of Jesus

Wear our stripes
In the belly of Jesus
Hold onto life
In the belly of Jesus

Blood on the floor
In the belly of Jesus

Spit on the shore
From the belly of Jesus

# The Enduring Resistance the Constant Affirmation

With all the power of us, the spirit and the muscle, the brain and the imagination, the will and the endurance we have steadily resisted the assault on our people while simultaneously affirming our humanity on our own terms from our own souls with our own voices wrapped in our own beautiful skin. We have planted our feet, marched into battle and fought our enemies. We have won battles and suffered setbacks but we have never retreated. We are a people undefeated, unconquered, here in this place we always resist and lift our Black lives up for ourselves first, but also for the world. We plant our feet and move forward. The future is our land.

*  *  *

There are two constant realities of African American life and every generation has carried them. First, Black people's lives and rights are negotiable within the boundaries of American democracy. In every period of US history, Black people have been betrayed by those who rule and govern through compromises with the most racist sector of the population for political and economic gain. African Americans hope for something different but know betrayal is not only possible but probable. It is always evident to varying degrees. In the current political climate with a president who is led by white supremacists and with a complicit national political leadership there is an open assault on Black lives and rights. Voter suppression, state and vigilante violence, defunding of public schools are amongst a growing list of attacks on Black people. Again, the betrayal.

Second, African Americans realize no one is coming for us. There is no historical evidence that any group or government, locally or nationally will voluntarily intervene forcefully enough to stop the contemporary version of the violent suppression of Black life. However, history does confirm that the African American community only moves forward when it protects and asserts its own interests. We have allies today and have had them in the past. Alliances occur where there are mutual interests. Those interests can be long or short term, they are not permanent. The responsibility for Black Liberation is our own. Only our own.

* * *

We, all of us, have an obligation to insure our resistance to injustice and oppression is known to each new generation.

# The Intractable Relationship

Africans were forced to the Americas for one purpose, to be super-exploited. In an atrocity of unimaginable violence and brutality, Africa's daughters and sons were kidnapped, tortured, sexually assaulted and murdered in a criminal enterprise and conspiracy to extract Africa's human and natural resources to produce unfathomable riches for the old rulers of Europe and the new rulers of the Americas. The Atlantic slave trade and the enslavement of Africans and their descendants was the foundation for an obscene redistribution and accumulation of wealth and power for the plantation class in the southern United States and their emerging capitalist counterparts and co-conspirators in the north. To perpetuate and justify this crime against Africans and humanity, a Euro-American narrative of inherent white superiority and innate Black inferiority was infused into all aspects of US culture and projected to all corners of the world.

The systematically and systemically imposed inferior condition of Black people as an unpaid labor force, as a commodity to be bought and sold and as vulnerable and cheap workers, established the foundational relationship between Black people and the US economy in both its private and public sector. That economic foundation has continued to this day to define the economic relationship of African Americans and US society which determines the political, legal and cultural relationship. Even after the defeat of the slave system, the exploitation of Black people has remained constant through theft of land and property, discriminatory hiring and lending, lower wages and special taxes through fines and penalties, private prisons and convict labor. In millions of transactions a day, the African American community is exploited in ways that are based upon the prevailing belief in American culture that Black people are a servant class who are only here for the benefit of wealthy white people and to make working class white people believe they have some innate superiority that trumps their poverty. In American culture, African Americans are simply a profit center that must be available for exploitation. We are reminded of this every day in small and large ways. The constant and consistent institutional exploitation and the imposition of a white supremacist narrative to justify it are the basis of an intractable relationship between African Americans and the country of our birth and choice.

The narrative of white supremacy was codified in law with the 3/5 compromise in the writing and ratification of the US constitution. That compromise amongst the founders allowed the criminal plantocracy of the south to increase and consolidate their power by allowing them to count Black men as 3/5 of a man in order to gain additional proportional congressional representation. The political power they accumulated from the beginning of the republic allowed them to protect and expand their criminal enterprise until it was broken in 1865 by the violence of the Civil War and defeated by the Union Army with 180,000 Black soldiers fighting for freedom. The power of the most racist forces of the south have continued to exist into the 21st century with only a brief interruption during the 12 years of Reconstruction.

The narrative of white supremacy was sanctioned and promulgated by the Southern Baptist church and other Christian organizations who supported slavery as the divine will of the Christian God. Their blessing and advocacy of white superiority and the enslavement of Black people laid the foundation for the church of Jim Crow and the contemporary right wing Christian evangelical movement. The relationship between those churches and the power of the blood descendants and the political descendants of the plantocracy continue to maintain the influence of the racist rightwing in the national political conversation and practice.

Both the Republican and Democratic parties have made unholy compromises with racism through deals and laws that facilitate the exploitation of the Black community. Voter suppression, housing and education policy, mandatory sentencing, suppression of labor rights and discrimination against African American farmers, support for exploitative banking practices and many, many other open and hidden, legal and illegal actions of the two parties perpetuate the exploitation of African Americans and the ideas and practices of white supremacy.

In recent years there have been numerous calls by political leaders, academics, artists and others for an "uncomfortable conversation on race in America." We should have those conversations. In fact, they are going on everywhere, from the classrooms of storied educational institutions to the pages and screens of modern media. Conversations about race will not, cannot, make the changes that are necessary to resolve the intractable relationship. As Martin Luther King, Jr. realized shortly before his death, to change the intractable relationship between African Americans and the US requires a "radical redistribution of economic and political power." Only then will African Americans live in a country that protects our human rights and honors and enforces our civil rights.

\* \* \*

# African Americans, Racist Counter Revolution, and Trump*

*there is no place on this earth without my fingerprint,
and my heel in the skeleton of skyscrapers, and my
sweat in the brilliance of diamonds![1]*

Africa's human and natural resources were extracted through atrocity to build the wealth of the white western world. The trans-Atlantic slave trade and European colonialism are the economic and cultural foundations of the global power of the white western world. To justify the atrocities of slavery and colonialism, a mythology was created, a story told, a culture built and governments created around the idea that Europeans and their descendants are superior to the rest of the world, especially Africans and their descendants. In the context of a traditionally white supremacist society like the United States, where white men have traditionally held power almost exclusively, it is not difficult to comprehend their ferocious opposition, the violent response to any idea or movement that challenges that authority. We are witnessing and experiencing it today.

From the first minute and every second of every minute since the atrocity began, we have been engaged in a long struggle, spanning generations, to free Black humanity from people and systems that deprecate us for the purpose of satisfying their greed or their need to assert dominance over us. Our history of resistance to oppression and our assertion of our humanity is the framework for contextualizing and organizing in the 21st century as it has been for all previous generations of African Americans. This knowing is critical in the storm of a white racist counter-revolution that culminated in the election of Trump and the takeover of the federal government by the right wing of the Republican Party.

The mythological political narrative of the United States begins with a story of noble ideas and noble white men creating a new nation where the human rights of all people would be respected. From that premise those noble men with noble ideas created a government of the people, for the people and by the people. They established law, policy and practice to

9

form a participatory and inclusive democracy, moving steadily toward a more perfect union.

Euro-descendant genocide against indigenous peoples to facilitate the theft of their land, the subjugation and exclusion of women and the enslavement of Africans and their descendants are some of the obvious problems with that narrative. Critical complications also exists in trying to reconcile the enterprise of slavery and the ideas of freedom when at significant moments in US history, times when those with power could have moved the country toward the idea of a government that respected and protected the human and civil rights of all people, they chose to do the opposite and preserve undeserved power and unwarranted profit.

Throughout the entire history of this country a significant and intransigent section of the white population vehemently opposes any attempt to create a legitimate, inclusive, participatory democracy, an equitable economy and a government dedicated to both human rights and civil rights. They rebel against any attempt to abolish the mythology and culture of white supremacy and the privileges it renders them, even if those privileges ultimately do not give the majority of them the resources or opportunities they desire and need for a better life. Rich and powerful white men have long understood that an appeal to white supremacist entitlement still resonates deeply within white America. The 2016 presidential campaign and election of Trump is the most recent proof. It is evidence of the temporary success of the white right-wing counter-revolt against the civil rights and social justice revolution that dismantled Jim Crow and has steadily pushed American culture, its public and private institutions, toward equitable inclusion and participation in the economic, political and social life of the country.

Historically, the tendency within the white community has been to acquiesce to the white supremacists while condemning their ideology. As with previous white right revolts, the success of the current revolt will be temporary, although it has the potential to have a negative impact for years or even generations. As an example, the consequences of conceding to the racist plantocracy in the founding of the US still reverberates in every aspect of society today.

The writing and ratification of the US Constitution was the first opportunity to create a governing structure on the basis of human rights codified as law. Instead, the founders of the United States chose to not only protect but promote the most egregious violation, the enslavement of Black people. The so-called 3/5 compromise was an agreement to engage in a scheme to protect and extend the power of the white plantation class in the south. The enslavers would be allowed to count African men as 3/5 of a man while also denying them any rights expressed in the new nation or its constitution. By falsely boosting eligible population figures in southern states the plantocracy was granted more representation in Congress, cementing their ability to protect their profits and their white supremacist culture. This practice continued through the Jim Crow era during which Black people were counted for political representation but denied the right to vote as well as other rights.

Instead of creating a polity with unequivocal, absolute opposition to slavery, the US constitution gave legal authorization and also cultural justification for a 77-year extension of slavery, a system that "…would disgrace a nation of savages." It was a system that brutalized African Americans while its perpetrators professed piety.

"Women are considered of no value, unless they continually increase their owner's stock. They are put on a par with animals. This same master shot a woman through the head, who had run away and been brought back to him. No one called him to account for it. If a slave resisted being whipped, the bloodhounds were unpacked, and set upon him, to tear his flesh from his bones. The master who did these things was highly educated, and styled a perfect gentleman. He also boasted the name and standing of a Christian, though Satan never had a truer follower.[1]

The 3/5 compromise was a constitutional embrace of white supremacist ideology and practice and deepened its infection into all American institutions and throughout its culture where it has remained intractable into the 21st century. As historian Gerald Horne points out, "Whatever the case, it is evident that there is a disjuncture between the supposed progressive and avant-garde import of 1776 and the worsening conditions for Africans and the indigenous that followed upon the triumph of the rebels." The US Constitution became the law of the new nation by betraying Black people. Slavery endured in the south and the north nursed on it with blood dripping from its mouth.

Reconstruction, that brief period immediately after the Civil War, presented the second major opportunity to turn toward a human rights based democratic society. It was born from the defeat of the plantocracy's attempt to establish a new confederate nation on the noble idea that slavery was God's divine order and Black people were created to serve white people. Their defeat was the result of a two and a half century, multifaceted resistance of Black people to American slavery, the support of indigenous and white allies and the violence of the Civil War which the north won with a Union Army that included 180,000 Black soldiers fighting for Black freedom.

Creating a new anti-slavery south, a democratic south where they could live as free people on the land they had cultivated for generations, finally felt possible for the African American community. The 13th, 14th and 15th Amendments seemed to present the potential to create a pathway into full first class citizenship for Black people. To exercise their rights as citizens, Black men registered to vote, ran for and were elected to local, state and national office. The newly free four million descendants of Africa pursued empowerment with education, guns from the war, land that many now owned, Reconstruction courts and laws that enforced their rights and a federal government that remained in the former confederate states to suppress the plantocracy. It seemed as if freedom fought for had finally been won.

The enslavement of Black people in the US and the colonies that preceded it lasted 246 years from 1619 to 1865. Reconstruction lasted 12 years, 1865 to 1877. The project to create a democratic south where the descendants of enslaved Africans would be equal citizens building a life for their families and a future for their children came to a terrifying end with the Tilden-Hayes Compromise. The contested presidential election of 1876 between Republican Rutherford B. Hayes and Democrat Samuel Tilden was resolved through a compromise between the two parties. Tilden conceded the presidency and Hayes agreed to withdraw federal troops from the former confederate states allowing the plantation class to retake power. When the troops left, the space they had occupied was filled with a 90 year reign of terror by white supremacist vigilantes like the KKK and southern state and local governments who enforced the subjugation of Black citizens. The power of rich white people to exploit and abuse them was restored and the monster Jim Crow ruled the south for the next nine decades with the explicit or implied complicity of US presidents, congress and the courts, churches, media and other institutions south and north, east and west. "The South resented giving the Afro-American his freedom, the ballot box and the Civil Rights Law." That resentment was evident in the rules, laws and customs to humiliate and remind Black people of their absolute vulnerability within the white supremacist system and their place beneath even the poorest, most ignorant white person. Black resistance deepened and continued, fashioning a conception of freedom for the future.

In the tradition, 20th century African Americans fought oppression on all fronts. By the mid-1950s through the 1970s the fight had created a movement with the unshakeable faith of Black ancestors, the unbreakable tradition of Black resistance and the unmovable force of a Black warrior generation determined to be free.

On Tuesday, November 4, 2008, African American democrat Barack Hussein Obama was elected president of the United States. With a broad coalition that included Hispanics, young people, Asian Americans, women and labor Obama won the election with 53% of the votes over Republican John McCain's 45%. At the center of the coalition were African Americans who cast 95% of their ballots for Obama. It was not the first time they were responsible for electing a Democratic president. John Kennedy ('60), LB Johnson ('64), Jimmy Carter ('76) and Bill Clinton

('92) all owe their elections to the overwhelming support of the Black community. The 2008 election was different, its meaning deeper and more powerful for Black people and for the United States.

The election of Barack Obama was a result of the long freedom movement of enslaved Africans and their descendants who stood and fought for centuries never accepting our dreadful condition as our destiny. His election was also directly the result of the impact of the political and social changes forced by the battles and victories of the Civil Rights/Black Power Movement and the consciousness of self-determination it created. Other movements, women, Hispanics, native peoples, LGBTQ communities, Asian Americans, young people were inspired by and often aligned with Black people who were also inspired by them. As those movements grew in strength and influence, American institutions were challenged to reject the old idea of this country as a white supremacists Christian nation and become more inclusive of all the Americans.

The social justice revolution and its movements forced changes in law, social practice, politics and culture. As a result, the United States of the 21st century does not look like the same country it was in 1950 when white men held almost all power exclusively and benefitted first and the most from available resources and opportunities. As the social movements won victories and challenged the culture, the privileged position of white men was diluted and their traditional structures of white supremacy were weakened. Civil rights, women's rights, LGBTQ rights, inclusiveness, recognition of a multi-cultural America and more equitable sharing of power enraged the white traditionalists, especially in the south. They pushed back and a counter-revolution grew with their discontent.

"White Democrats will desert their party in droves the minute it becomes a Black party." Leaders of the Republican Party saw the outrage of southern Democrats as their party under Kennedy and Johnson was forced by the Civil Rights Movement to oppose segregation. Understanding the growing white opposition to Black empowerment, Republicans welcomed them with assurances they would uphold traditional white American values. Nixon spoke to and for those he called the silent majority. Later, Ronald Reagan solidified their loyalty by assuring them when he launched his 1980 campaign for president in Philadelphia, Mississippi the site where civil rights workers James Chaney, Mickey Schwerner and Andrew Goodman were murdered in 1964 assisting Black people registering to vote. Reagan spoke nostalgically about the old south and proclaimed his preference for states' rights (a battle cry of confederate apologists and segregationists) confirming to the supporters of the old America, the defenders of the old white power, that Reagan would help them take their country back.

At the time of Reagan's 1980 election, the growing strength of the white counter-revolution was evident in politics but not yet powerful enough to take and hold control of the federal government. Reagan was president for two terms and pushed the agenda forward. The Republican Party embraced the right wing counter-revolution, even convincing the less conservative members that they could win elections by appealing to the white discontent. The Republicans supported and mounted legal challenges to affirmative action. They developed and supported the "culture wars" launched by the white Christian evangelical movement and public campaigns to challenge ethnic studies programs and diversity in education, Hispanic immigration and multi-culturalism and attacked women's reproductive rights. They became skilled at propaganda, built networks of speakers, launched talk radio and television programs that appealed to white racist discontent and relentlessly attacked the progress of the social revolution. Slowly, state by state, they elected candidates who promised fidelity to their cause. They captured positions on school boards, county commissions, city councils, state legislatures, governorships and congress. They also elected two presidents, both named Bush, neither hard right but both willing to placate the hard right wing to get elected.

In 1984 and '88, Jesse Jackson ran for the Democratic nomination for president and although he didn't secure enough votes, he succeeded in pushing the Democratic Party to remain committed to a platform that was more aligned with the past demands of the social justice movement agenda.

Between the two Bushes, Bill Clinton was elected president as a centrist in the Democratic Party and began to pull the platform from the left and toward the center right. Before his tenure as president ended and with his wife and political adviser Hillary, he led the country to accept a culture of mass incarceration that devastated African American communities across the US and fed the racists' narrative of the necessity to manage Black people through violence. It was a revitalization of the narrative created during slavery to justify the brutalization of enslaved Black people.

In 2001 George W. Bush was handed the presidency over Al Gore by the Supreme Court in a contested election, it was a signal of the growing strength of the Republican right-wing. They were marching steadily toward an ultimate goal, control of the entire federal government to enact their right wing agenda. Meanwhile the Black social justice movement was no longer leading a powerful united front making change. The coalition was trying to defend what had been won but didn't have the deep national grassroots movement that had been the foundation of social justice change. Veteran and emerging organizers, were in communities working heroically everywhere, but not with the national effectiveness of the previous period. Meanwhile, the Republican right was consolidating and expanding its power on the local and state level. They gerrymandered congressional districts, launched a national strategy to dismantle the Voting Rights Act and implemented a strategy to suppress African American voting rights.

The 2008 presidential campaign represented a confrontation of the political and social forces that had been struggling over America's future. The Civil Rights/Black Power movement had successfully challenged the old order of white supremacy and along with other social movements had pulled the US from its past and toward a future possibility of an inclusive participatory democracy. The candidacy and campaign of Barack Obama galvanized progressive forces in a way that had not been seen in a long time. The united front, a broad coalition of many different interests, came together around an agenda of change to elect the first African American president of the United States and send the first African American family to live in the White House.

African Americans rightly felt enormous pride in an experience that represented a victory in our long, continued struggle to be citizens in the country of our birth and choice. For us, Barack and Michelle were a familial and familiar part of our story. Representing the arc of our striving, they were a Black woman and man grown from the foundation, the complex bottom of color and class. They were our people succeeding at the highest levels while facing seemingly insurmountable odds. To many they carried the spirit of the Black national anthem: "full of the faith that the dark past has taught us...full of the hope that the present has brought us."[2]

We basked briefly in the hope that the unique moment represented a new day for us, for this country, for the future. We had little time to ponder the possibilities because shortly after the election our historical memory coughed up the reality of the relationship between America and its African American citizens. With every victory, in every generation, we are always acutely aware of the specter of white supremacy, its violent manifestations standing in the shadows sharpening its teeth, looming long and large in our consciousness. Within hours after the 2008 election, it leapt from the shadows and a surge of the ugly truth began to roll in and over the possibility that this country was ready and willing to break with its past.

> Cross burnings. Schoolchildren chanting 'Assassinate Obama.' Black figures hung from nooses. Racial epithets scrawled on homes and cars. Incidents around the country referring to President-elect Barack Obama are dampening the postelection glow of racial progress and harmony, highlighting the stubborn racism that remains in America.[3]

In the wake of Obama's election, the Southern Poverty Law Center expressed hope and issued a warning:

> Even as we embark on a new national adventure, the signs are worrying. It may be that the hatemongers are wrong, that Americans' better angels will prevail and the changes that are sweeping America will not result in a growing rage on the right. But experience tells us that while we hope for the

best, we also must prepare for what could be a dangerous, racially motivated backlash of hate.[4]

Black people braced for the storm we knew was coming, whisper-
ing concern that the mysterious racist "they" would assassinate Obama. Or
that the violence of racism would become a pandemic again, a sickness
growing strong enough to spread quickly. We heard the Republican pledge
to destroy the Obama presidency, to insure its failure. We saw the open disrespect by white elected officials and the growing hate in traditional and
social media directed at the Obamas including their daughters. We understood it was not about them as individuals it was about us, Black people,
collectively. They were the easy target, the obvious symbols of our struggle
for civil and human rights and they, we had to be denigrated, diminished,
damned. We witnessed Trump lead a racist campaign questioning our le-
gitimacy as US citizens by challenging President Obama's citizenship and
we could smell the putrid breath of the ante-bellum Supreme Court as it
read its Dred Scott decision:

> In the opinion of the Court the legislation and histories of the times, and
> the language used in the Declaration of Independence, show that neither
> the class of persons who had been imported as slaves nor their descendants,
> whether they had become free or not, were then acknowledged as a part of
> the people nor intended to be included in the general words used in that
> memorable instrument....They had for more than a century before been re-
> garded as beings of an inferior order and altogether unfit to associate with
> the white race, either in social or political relations; and so far inferior that
> they had no rights which the white man was bound to respect; and that the
> Negro might justly and lawfully be reduced to slavery for his benefit. He
> was bought and sold and treated as an ordinary article of merchandise and
> traffic whenever a profit could be made by it. This opinion was at that time
> fixed and universal in the civilized portion of the white race...."[5]

During the campaign of 2008, the Republican Party objective was not just
to win the presidency but to expand its dominance over the entire federal
government. They wanted the majority in both houses of congress, the presidency and a majority on the Supreme Court. They understood that they

could not succeed unless the network of right wing activists and donors were fully committed. Their presidential candidate John McCain, in his ambition to be president at all costs, was willing to compromise with the racist right wing by signaling, like his predecessors Nixon, Reagan and both Bushes that he and the modern Republican Party were committed to support their agenda if elected. Although McCain had been seen and touted as a maverick senator unwilling to fall in lock step with peers in his party, that image was shattered when he chose Sarah Palin, the right wing governor of Alaska, as his running mate. McCain lost to Obama. Although he was ultimately defeated by a significant margin, losing both the popular vote and the Electoral College, McCain had unleashed the ugly racist right wing elements of the Republican Party and called them to the surface.

McCain's compromise, backed by the Republican establishment, elevated Sarah Palin and the racist right wing of the Republican Party to a position of national acceptance as a legitimate and public force in American politics. That group organized themselves into the Tea Party and in 2010 sent more than 80 of their movement to Congress. Determined to dismantle every gain of the social justice movements and destroy the legacy of the first Black president, they helped Republicans capture the House of Representatives where they not only waged war against the Democrats but also those moderate Republicans who opposed them.

By the 2012 election, there was no longer a moderate Republican voice being heard. As in the past, they conceded power to the most racist elements of American politics. Republicans in the center either left congress or shut-up and fell in step with the right wing. Sarah Palin helped give voice to them but she could not lead them. A megalomaniacal real estate developer and reality TV personality with wealth and a high media profile, could. Donald Trump took over the task of promoting the lie that President Obama was not an American, endearing himself to Nazi's, white nationalists, Tea partyers, evangelical Christians, and others in the alternative right. He became their leader and he prepared to lead them into Washington D.C. after President Obama left office.

The election of Barack Obama and his relationship to Black liberation veterans is complex. It has to be understood in relationship to the relative strength or weakness of the Black liberation movement, the political forces vying for power in society and especially for control of the instruments of power. Obama is a center-left Democrat. There is a drastic difference between him and the racist right-wing which is evident now. In discussing the 2012 re-election campaign Angela Davis said, "We learned a lot from that election. It was actually quite incredible. Even more so than the first election. During the first election most people were myopically focused on the individual who was the candidate, right? This time around, many of us were really afraid that the Republican candidate would win, which would mean disaster with respect to political issues." His election was clearly important to African Americans and others in the coalition that elected him. He was also president of the American imperialist empire. Analyzing the phenomenon of his election and his presidency is important to our understanding of how to organize against the counter-revolution.

The 2012 reelection of President Obama demonstrated that the coalition that elected him in '08 had held in the presidential race but was steadily losing in state and congressional races. Shortly after the second Obama inauguration we begin to see the forces that had been unleashed. We felt it first when an American teenager walking down an American street, eating American candy on the way to his American family's home, is stalked and murdered by a racist vigilante. A Black son was dead, and there was no justice for his family. A wave of Black deaths, lynchings, murders of African American women and men followed. In our grief we were reminded of a history that was not the past. In the second decade of the 20th century a Black person was being killed every 28 hours at the hands of the police or vigilantes.

It wasn't just the vigilante murder of Trayvon or the jail hanging of Sandra Bland or the police shooting of Mike Brown. It wasn't blood spilt on the floor of our church and hymnal. It wasn't the violence against all those children and all those women and all those men and all that agony and all those tears of all those families grieving in all those communities all over this country. It wasn't all those lies and all those excuses and all those people who choose to subvert justice. It wasn't all those anonymous cowardly hateful, white people who killed by telephone when they called the police to falsely report Black people with toy guns or walking suspiciously. It wasn't social media that allowed us access to the images and video and live streams of bloody assaults on Black bodies. It wasn't the brutes choking us, punching and kicking our elders, slamming our partners into concrete. It wasn't schools handcuffing our children, body slamming our girls and shocking our boys with Tasers. It wasn't were we lived or how much education we had or whether we were poor or rich. It was the bile of America's history retching into 21st century Black life.

Our rising anxiety grew in proportion to our increasing rage because we knew what this was. We understood instinctively that evident in our historical presence in America was the unrelenting violence we'd experienced for centuries and in the grief caused by every incident of state violence and each vigilante attack we saw the old scars we wore on our backs, our minds and on our souls. We knew this 21st century escalation was the sickening sound of a quickening all-out war on Black people. It was also being waged on women, people of color, non-Euro immigrants, Muslims. We knew what it was, American capitalism, especially its most right wing racist elements, depends upon the mythology of white supremacy.

We could feel this ghost rising up from the basements and creeping from the closets of families yearning for an American past that granted them an unearned and undeserved privilege. It was the racist army of southern slavers and northern accomplices rising up from the underworld where it had retreated to regroup from the battles it lost to the African American mass movement for Civil Rights and Black Power. It was America's institutional power aligning to assault us, again. It was James Weldon Johnson reminding us, "We have come over a way that with tears has been watered. We have come, treading our path through the blood of the slaughtered."

Contrary to the racist narrative of passive acceptance of our oppression, Black people resisted and fought enslavement, Jim Crow and every other form of oppression from the first day, the first minute of contact with those intent to steal our humanity. From the 1950s into the 1970s their descendants stood up in the spirit of those resisters and liberators and formed a mighty army that marched on the bastions of our oppression. The warrior generation, thousands of women and men, domestic workers and laborers, teachers, sharecroppers and preachers, students, artists and lawyers, elders, parents and children engaged in battle after battle for justice in what came to be known as the Civil Rights/Black Power Movement. They joined or formed the NAACP, SCLC, CORE, SNCC, the Mississippi Freedom Democratic Party, Women's Civic organizations, the Black Guards of Monroe North Carolina, the Deacons for Defense in Louisiana and the Lowndes County Freedom Organization (the Black Panther Party in Alabama). They created the Revolutionary Action Movement and the League of Black Revolutionary Workers, the Black Panther Party for Self Defense, the Us Organization, the Republic of New Afrika, the Congress of African People and the African Liberation Support Committee. They held Black Power Conferences and convened the National Black Political Convention. They forced American education to include Black people's story through their own eyes and demanded an end to sexist and patriarchal ideas in society and within the Black Freedom Movement. They created the Black Arts Movement, drafted the Gary Declaration and the Cohambee River Collective Statement. They challenged the legal forces of oppression and discrimination, worked in the labor movement, built independent institutions of education, culture and politics. Opened clinics and community organizations. Reclaimed and reconnected our consciousness with Africa and demanded its importance be recognized. We called ourselves beautifully Black and African American, claiming both histories and experiences. And there was progress. We had dismantled Jim Crow, transferred power to our communities, educated more Black people than ever before and grew a college educated middle class. Black people broke down discriminatory barriers in the public and private sector, became mayors and elected representatives to congress, built businesses and climbed into the executive level of corporations. With the election of Obama it seemed as if that progress would eventually lead to an eradication of the white supremacist foundation of American culture. We were wrong. While we had rightly focused on consolidating and expanding the gains of our struggle, the warrior generation was aging and our battle tested organizations in civil rights and Black liberation had also aged, weakened or no longer existed. We were not ready for war, but there were people working for social justice in communities and building organizations. In our mobilization in the Obama campaigns we were also preparing.

The 21st century counter-revolution of white supremacist capitalism had begun marshalling their forces 40 years ago. Their strategy to retake power and to "take our country back" included an above ground plan using the legal structure, politics and vast sums of money from sectors of the billionaire class to create institutions, non-profits, think tanks and organizations advancing the take america back agenda. It also included an underground mobilization of white supremacist groups that were not yet able to come out of the shadows. They would emerge in the 2016 presidential campaign, but not on the fringes, in the center of the Republican primaries and then more forcefully in the Trump campaign.

The growing assertion of the white right presence, the rise in state and vigilante violence against Black people and the hardened opposition to the Obama administration put African Americans on the defensive. We begin organizing in our mourning and marching and making our way to where we knew it was going. We'd seen it coming, building since 2008 and the election of Obama. The violence, the rise of racism in the public discourse, the continuing surge of mass incarcerations, the permission given by politicians to openly denigrate Black people. And if we were confused about it, we could see it on social media or talk shows every day. We knew it was coming, the storm that is never still inside of us. It is sometimes held back, hidden beneath hope it will not be necessary to feel it explode beyond our grief, our tears our generations of scars passed on in the quiet discussions of how to stay alive when being hunted by ogres. We knew it was coming, beyond our reasoning and theory, beyond our prayers and attempts at reconciliation, it was coming, an explosion of unstoppable force, the heat that races through our blood into our brains reminding us that there is no one else, there is nothing else except our own fire that can back up these monsters. They called it out and it came roaring with courage, conviction and commitment from young voices and old wisdom. "Black Lives Matter!" the sisters said as they gather and lead us to build new armies. In Jackson, MS and in Newark, NJ the Black radical tradition of grassroots organizing was the foundation of the successful mayoral campaigns of Chokwe Lumumba and Ras Baraka. A new movement has been taking shape and learning, growing from protest to governing to the structural changes that Martin Luther King called for.

The election of Trump shocked many in 2016. But it is not sudden or accidental. It is the successful realization of the white counter-revolution strategy. It is the product of a history that makes the choice to betray Black people, women and others in favor of a white male power and narrative. By 2016 the white supremacist counter-revolution had gained enough strength to capture the federal government. They control the White House, both houses of Congress and the Supreme Court. They also have control over all federal agencies, the military and the state department. Nazi's, the KKK and other terrorists are in and now have access to the White House and openly parade around the internet and in communities carrying confederate flags and torches. They don't have to hide and they will not retreat unless forced to. They believe Trump and his sycophants are all powerful. They are not.

As with the birther movement, Trump and his band of racists are furiously attempting to attack the power and accomplishments of the African American community by eradicating any legacy of President Obama. Executive orders from Trump rain from the White House pushing back environmental protections and consumer protections against bankers. Attorney General Sessions has ordered the Justice Department to seek maximum penalties against drug offenders taking the country back to policies that led to the mass incarceration of Black and Brown people. Republicans are silently complicit with the destruction of health care and public education. There is a huge surge in open racist acts of violence and attacks on multi-cultural education and inclusion. The right wing wants war and Trump is a warmonger seeking to make himself look powerful by sending the daughters and sons of Americans who are not his children to war. The Trump administration is filled with criminals engaged in all manner of criminal enterprises. They look all powerful but they are not.

Black people and our allies are in a fight for the future of this country, again. We have to build a broad united front that includes every sector of the African American community around an agenda of our concerns and objectives. We have to build a broad united front with our allies around an agenda that includes our concerns and objectives. We are in a fight not unlike the one to end slavery which seemed invincible. We are in a fight not unlike the one to defeat Jim Crow and other forms of oppression in the 20th century. We must organize in every way necessary including protests, elections and other methods. We will win. White supremacy is a lie. The people and structures that depend on it will be defeated by the truth.

*"Truth is on the side of the oppressed..."* Malcolm X

*First published in: *Not Our President: New Directions from the Pushed Out, the Others, and the Clear Majority in Trump's Stolen America* (Third World Press Foundation, 2017).

# Notes on Black Women

Black women have always led us, we have not always acknowledged their leadership which amounts to a type of narrative theft. It is not only an inconsistency within any movement for justice, it is injustice. Our struggle is for human rights, civil rights and self-determination for all of us.

\* \* \*

The degradation of Black women in the Black male narrative in popular culture must not be acceptable even if the beat is banging. We can't keep dancing to the sound of violence against Black women by the police, the courts, the prisons and by the men who are supposed to love them.

\* \* \*

In discussing gender role beliefs in my African American Sstudies classes, I ask the students who are overwhelmingly Black, if they believe men should be the head of the house? The majority of them, both women and men say yes. The follow-up, "give a reason that doesn't include God" meaning not derived from their faith beliefs. This is where they have difficulty. The men assert the necessity of male leadership because they are supposed to protect the women and children and provide for them. Why? Are women incapable of protecting the family and providing? We know that is not true. They respond, "It is the way it has always been and the natural order of things. It says so in the Bible or in traditional African societies, they claim." Ahhh, we are back to God said so. The women who agree respond similarly that men are supposed to provide and protect and they too revert to religious justification. Some don't need God as explanation, because it is more a preference which they explain as having a man to take out the trash, put gas in their car, and mow the lawn. Man stuff they say. They also imply that it is often the price of companionship. In every class there are also women and men, more women than men, who oppose the idea that men by virtue of biology should be designated head of the house.

"Is there something in men that makes them better decision makers?" I ask. To that question the women laugh loudly and give a resounding no. After we have drawn out all of the justifications and the opposition to whether men should be head of the household, I ask a final question of the women in the class: "How many of you have been taught by your mother, grandmother, aunt or some other woman that you must make men believe they are the head of the household knowing they really aren't?" This question also elicits laughter and confession that the majority of the women in the class have been given that strategy and do not really believe in inherent male leadership. It comes as a surprise to the men but many of them accept the truth that in most of our families and institutions, the women not only hold it together but lead the decision making process.

\* \* \*

That exercise is how we begin to study and discuss the suppression of Black women's voice, thinking and leadership in the herstory and history of our struggle for liberation.

\* \* \*

There have always been women and some men committed to pulling Black women from the shadows of history to raise up herstory and situate them as central in our lives and struggle, to learn from them and honor their contributions. One of the most important developments today is the rapidly expanding research and scholarship on Black women in the liberation movement from a new generation of scholars, artists and activists. They are reshaping our thinking, practice and teaching. We have to expand it into every aspect of our lives.

\* \* \*

This generation is creating a new political language and understanding for confronting and ending violence against women. Led by young women, they demand and end to and greater protection against sexual assault and domestic violence, but also that our community embrace the responsibility to teach boys not to assault women. They demand we understand the existence of what they have termed rape culture and that men and the Black community fight it with the fearlessness and commitment we fight other forms of violence and injustice.

When marriage equality was before the Supreme Court, I asked my students who opposed it and to give a reason that was not because of their faith tradition. Usually those against it could not explain their opposition outside of an interpretation of their God's law. When asked if the state (government) sanctions marriage, is it acceptable to have two sets of laws, They answered no, although some still said it is not right in the eyes of their God. As we pressed the issue of the government legitimizing marriage for some citizens but not for others, they begin to understand it as a civil rights issue. The government cannot apply the law to some citizens and not to others. This discussion helped expand their understanding of the Civil Rights Movement and its demand that the government treat all citizens equally.

# Notes on State and Vigilante Violence

When police harass, attack or kill Black people it is the government violating the rights of its citizens without due process and through extra-legal violence. Whether it is the action of an individual officer or the policy and practice of a department, the police are agents of the government. Illegal stops, searches, arrests, violence and murder are declarations that Black people are not protected by the Constitution and therefore can be accused, tried, convicted, punished or executed on the street. Throughout US history, the extra-judicial relationship between the police and the Black community has been affirmed by the willingness of white Americans to accept the violations of the citizenship rights of African Americans. Deeply rooted in US culture is the white supremacist lie that Black people are inherently inferior and pre-disposed to criminality which necessitates the use of violence to manage us. While many white people may find this morally repugnant and against their political values, the unfortunate reality is that rarely does their empathy reach the level of indignation and action in response to the widespread and continued violent desecration of the citizenship of African Americans.

\* \* \*

We have to stop allowing and using the racist term Black on Black crime. We must demand the media cease using it also. It is racist because only the African American community has crime described in racial terms. News outlets never report a crime in white communities committed by white people as white on white crime. Black on Black crime implies that Black people have a genetic disposition to criminality. There is nothing unusual about Black people being victims of crime committed by other Black people. Most crime is committed based on proximity. In other words if you live in a white community you are more likely to have crime committed by white people. This is true for every community whose population is primarily one group. Whenever you hear a news reporter use Black on Black crime, call, email, text and demand they stop or begin describing white people's

29

crime as white on white or white on humanity for the past several centuries.

\* \* \*

In the wake of so many murders, a seemingly endless roll call, Trayvon Martin, Aura Rosser, Jordan Davis, Tanisha Anderson, Sandra Bland, Eric Garner, Philando Castille…a pool of tears and a hymn of weeping baptizes us almost every day. The 2017 president and attorney general have given the order to ratchet up state suppression of Black people and given the signal to white racists to increase their attacks. Black people and those who believe in justice must be prepared to respond.

\* \* \*

July 13, 2013 (George Zimmerman was acquitted for the murder of Trayvon Martin) Tonight we had a hard lesson, a bitter reminder that a Black life is still not valued in this society and our people are still vulnerable to being lynched. We must never stop fighting for justice and make sure every generation, every person knows they have a sacred obligation to contribute to this fight in whatever way they can.

\* \* \*

The Zimmerman trial for the murder of Trayvon Martin was a farce and the not guilty verdict is the continuation of 20 generations of legal justification for lynching African Americans. There are no circumstances today or in the history of the United States where an African American man can stalk, accost and murder a white teenage boy, (especially in the south) and the police not arrest him (or shoot him on the spot). There are no circumstances today or in the history of this country where an African American man can tell 4 white teenage boys in a car to turn their loud music down and when they don't respond as directed the man gets a gun out of his glove compartment loads it and shoots into their car killing one of them and then casually drives away, never calls 911, leaves town the next day with some bullshit story and not be the target of a national manhunt. As we know, in real life cases where Black boys and girls were murdered, justice was not done. We also know if it had been Black men shooting white teens, the Black men would have been hunted, captured, arrested or killed, tried and convicted and sentenced to spend the rest of their lives in prison or hell.

\* \* \*

The notion that the criminals who murdered Trayvon and Jordan did so out of fear is both ahistorical and nonsense to justify racist criminal behavior. These acts of violence do not occur out of fear; they occur out of hatred born from a white supremacist father and a white supremacist beneficiary mother. Going back centuries there is documentation that this country has an extensive and long record of promoting hatred against Africans and their descendants to justify the heinous crimes committed to satisfy the greed of those who exploit us.

\* \* \*

The history of the US and the current climate of violence against African Americans suggests the Stand Your Ground Laws will become much less appealing to most Americans if Black people, with a long record of justifiable fear of being killed by white people, begin to stand our ground.

\* \* \*

Trayvon Martin, Darnisha Harris, Aiyana Stanley-Jones, Jordan Davis and Tamir Rice remind us this is still a dangerous place for our children because there are still sick people who hate them because they were born so beautifully Black. The state murder of our children reminds us that our struggle for a just society where our children can be wholly who they are is our responsibility, some may join us, but it is ours as a family, as a community, as a people, as a nation.

I'm sick of the lies, not fooled by the tears of politicians, don't believe the apologies, can't accept the false contrition. People who murder and support racist violence against Black people and hide behind excuses are liars and cowards. The racist who openly declares his /her white supremacist sickness as the reason for their terroristic violence is unfortunately amongst the few who are willing to tell the truth about the core belief of millions in this country. The struggle continues.

\* \* \*

We understand that the forces of capitalism and white supremacy are driving rising police repression against the Black community. Given our analysis we are now faced with the crucial task of developing an agenda, program, and political instruments that give us greater capability to define, fight for and win our demands. If we don't define what we are for then we are left having rage driven discussion about systemic and systematic repression and exploitation and what we are against, leaving us constantly on the defensive with minimum capacity for transformative struggle and few victories.

\* \* \*

Some people believe they can abuse us, commit violence and murder against us and there will be no consequences. They are grossly mistaken. Justice is always enroute and when it arrives it does not always appear as one would expect.

\* \* \*

Remember Sandra Bland! Obviously, neither law nor the god these killers claim to follow is powerful enough to stop the murder of Black people by vigilantes in or out of uniform. We have to face two indisputable facts. First, the political, legal, religious, social, educational and economic culture of the US has always accepted and been complicit in violence against Black people. Second, people continue to assault us, violate us and murder us, because they know there are no consequences. When we accept these facts we will act accordingly.

\* \* \*

I say it again. The police and vigilantes murder Black people because they know there are few or no consequences.

\* \* \*

As we continue to gather ourselves in the wake of the continued government sanctioned and perpetrated terrorism against our community, we must also remember that in our entire history in this country we have never accepted or been defeated by oppression, violence or attempts to deny our humanity. Our history confirms the power of Black people is most effective when we are organized to assert our human and civil rights.

\* \* \*

In the face of the rise of racist repression and violence against Black people various people keep calling for a conversation on race. It is not a conversation on race that is needed to understand the great divide in the US. It is a conversation about citizenship and the meaning it has for different groups of Americans. It is a conversation about a government that has facilitated the repression of Black people because the fundamental relationship that we have with this country is one of exploitation and disenfranchisement reinforced by violence. Even with the election of an African American president the relationship with the government did not improve, it got worse. The systematic and sinister conspiracy of the Republican Party to suppress Black voter, its determination to ramp up racist language and imagery in the public discourse are all to remind the confederate flag wavers that this is a white man's country and Black people are only here to serve their needs.

\* \* \*

All American citizens should be outraged that government agencies are attacking and murdering American citizens. We regularly criticize human and civil rights violations in other countries yet there is a general silence of white political leadership on the increasing violence against American citizens. Thus the need for the conversation, are Black people and other people of color citizens in this country? Where is the proof that all citizens are treated equal and afforded equal protection under the law? There is no proof. Modern technology and social media have allowed the whole world to see what Black people already knew. Americans understand that, it has long been known in the Black community but cell phones with cameras and social media have now made it public, undeniable and yet there is still no outcry in the white community about government agencies attacking and murdering and illegally and unjustly incarcerating millions of US citizens.

# Notes on Martin Luther King and King Day Celebrations

Martin Luther King Jr. when called to serve, called to lead, called to sacrifice he answered the call. Are we listening?

\* \* \*

Martin Luther King Jr fought for justice for those with the least resources and the least power. So for those who are upset that streets named after him are usually in the most distressed communities remember that is where he would be doing his work if he were alive today. Streets named to honor Dr. King should be in the worst neighborhoods to remind us the work he committed his life to isn't finished.

\* \* \*

4/4/2014

46 years ago Dr. Martin Luther King was assassinated on the balcony of the Lorraine Hotel. He went to Memphis to support striking sanitation workers who wanted a living wage and respect as human beings. He was also in the midst of planning and launching the Poor Peoples Campaign to force the nation to address the issue of poverty, income inequality and resource distribution. The fight for a living wage, respect and ending poverty continues. Remember that Dr. King, the one who stood with working people and was more than a dreamer.

\* \* \*

On this day, this national holiday honoring our great ancestor Dr. Martin Luther King Jr. we honor him for both his contribution to the movement for freedom and as a symbol of those many women, men and children whose names we don't know but who also made tremendous sacrifices for justice. On this holiday, won through the struggle of millions under the leadership of Coretta Scott King, Stevie Wonder and others, it is our sacred responsibility and mission to insure the thought, work and message of Dr. King is not diminished by the forces within society who posture as if they admire and support his ideas, when in fact they are violently committed to the opposite. On this day let is remember and teach what Dr. King criticized and opposed as the triple evils of this society racism, militarism and poverty. On this day let us remember he stood with sanitation workers, went to jail alongside domestic workers and laborers, marched with under-educated children, activated artists to lend their creativity, learned from and walked with college students, called on clergy to act and gave all he had to our movement. On this day let us remember and teach his message of Black pride and psychological liberation and of the humanity of all of us. Let us preach his understanding of the Christian gospel: serve, uplift and empower the least of these. On this day let us remember and honor Dr. King. On this day, let us remember as our sisters and brothers said in Mozambique, "A Luta Continua!" "The Struggle Continues!"

* * *

January 16, 2017 first MLK Day after the election of Trump – and a shameful parade of Black celebrities make their pilgrimage to Trump Tower.

On this MLK day it is important to remember that in the course of a movement for justice those seeking to wrest power from those who oppress them have moments when their efforts through a variety of campaigns and methods force negotiations to transfer power to improve the conditions of their lives. This is one of the great lessons of the civil rights movement. The mass struggle, the sacrifices, the campaigns for civil and human rights disrupted segregated society and its capitalist transactions to a point where negotiating could take place. That is not the same thing as individual so called Black celebrities crawling to Trump Tower to kiss the ring and the ass of the tyrant whose ideas, policies, practice and intention is to wrest power and progress from us and others who have fought for generations to transform this country into a place where we can live as human beings. It is a question of where you stand, who you stand with and what you stand for.

*"The artist must elect to fight for slavery or freedom. I have made my choice." Paul Robeson*

Dr. Martin Luther King, Jr began his public ministry in Montgomery in 1955 standing with domestic workers and laborers, the cooks and the janitors. His public ministry was ended in Memphis 13 years later while standing with sanitation workers. In those 13 years he put aside the privileged life he could have enjoyed. Instead he chose to be of service to the cause of freedom.

# Notes on Malcolm X – Remembrances on His Birth and Death
## May 19, 1925 – February 21, 1965

Remembering Malcolm X and those who are incarcerated and the families that love and need them. Laid low by racism, hatred and ignorance Malcolm was an miseducated, violent criminal condemned to the dungeons of America. He flew high with education, truth, love and purpose. His life reminds us we cannot, should not write off the tremendous potential of each person. We can't afford to write anyone off. We can't afford to do without their gifts. When we write off a sister or brother in prison, on drugs, at a low point in their life, we should remember that Malcolm Little had rise to become Malcolm X one of the most influential figures of the 20th century.

\* \* \*

May 19 is the birthday of Malcolm Little Malcolm X Malik Shabazz who taught us that we can rise from the lowest to the highest and reminding us that we cannot give up on our children. Or ourselves.

\* \* \*

"By Any Means Necessary" is the most popular quote of Malcolm X. Unfortunately, it has obscured the more important phrase that precedes it: "We declare our right to be a human being, to be given the rights of a human being in this society, on this earth, in this day which we intend to bring about by any means necessary!" No one else can do it for us. We have to declare it demand it fight for it and build the will and capacity to bring it about. And all of us have to do what we can when we can to contribute to what the historian Vincent Harding called that great river of our history flowing toward justice. If we do that our children will be less vulnerable to the belief they are powerless and their generation will discover their mission and those who believe we have no right to our full humanity will be defeated again and again as they have in the past.

\* \* \*

Islam came to America in the bottom of a slave ship and has been practiced continuously since the period of enslavement despite attempts to suppress it. The most famous Muslims in American history are Malcolm X and his student Muhammad Ali.

\* \* \*

Today, May 19, 2015 we remember that 90 years ago a boy was born who changed the world. We came to know him as Malcolm X after he'd climbed up out of the racism, poverty and ignorance, self-hatred, criminality and incarceration that this system expected would crush or kill him like so many others. Malcolm X taught us that we have to transform ourselves to transform our world. We must love each other and ourselves. We must respect ourselves and each other. We must educate ourselves and each other. We must clean ourselves up and clean up our communities. He taught us, using his own life as a lesson, that we are greater than that which has been imposed upon us and when we free ourselves no one and nothing can make or keep us enslaved. Remember the lessons of Malcolm X as we imagine and create a humane world.

\* \* \*

51 years ago today Malcolm X was assassinated by forces who mistakenly thought they could kill him.

\* \* \*

*"We declare our right on this earth...to be a human being, to be respected as a human being, to be given the rights of a human being in this society, on this earth, in this day, which we intend to bring into existence by any means necessary."* - MX

# Notes on Standing Rock and Standing Together

26 states in the US have names from the languages of the indigenous peoples, those who were here before the European colonists arrived. All over this country their languages are represented as the names of rivers, lakes, roads and mountain passages. The question we never consider is where are those people, the ones who inhabited the land where there languages act as historical artifacts, a symbol that they were once here, a sign that something terrible happened. We go through our days, our weeks, our public and private lives never thinking about them or the ethnic cleansing and genocide committed against the many nations and speakers of the languages that are now draped across signposts and billboards welcoming visitors. It is one of the two great sins that continue to define the culture of America, genocide against the indigenous people to steal their land, enslavement of Africans to steal their labor.

\* \* \*

In 2016 the struggle at Standing Rock against the Dakota Access Pipeline brought to the public consciousness the on-going struggle of native peoples to live with dignity and the resources necessary for development and opportunity. The DAPL struggle also reminded us that we need to join together whenever and wherever possible in solidarity. Many people felt deflated by the Trump administration decision to allow the pipeline to go forward. We have to remember the struggle for the future of this country is a complex and long struggle. There will be many battles and some we will lose but history confirms the people move forward. We will win this war for the future. We are stronger because of the courageous people, our sisters and brothers, at Standing Rock! There is no defeat only lessons.

\* \* \*

The USA is not a white straight male Christian nation. Never has been, never will be. It has always been a country of women and men, many languages, religions, cultures and colors, sexual orientation and identity. A component and result of the long struggle of oppressed and marginalized peoples in this country is the correcting of US history to include all of the people. This was the basic premise behind Carter G Woodson creating "Negro History Week" which became Black History Month. Correcting US history and redefining the future to include all the Americans is also the central motivation of African American Studies, Women and Gender Studies, Hispanic and Islamic Studies. All which came about from students, faculty and communities demanding the stories and cultures of people of color and women be included in American education. There are those who are vehemently opposed to multi-cultural education, the teaching of US history and culture that includes all the Americans. Amongst them is the Republican Party which is attempting to pass legislation in several states to ban the teaching of the multi-cultural America. If education does not represent what America really is, another generation of white children are raised with a white supremacist view of their country and another generation of all the other Americans will grow up in a country that resembles the past. We will not and cannot go back. History is made by forward motion

# Black Community Dance

Trains rumble
both sides
of the tracks

languages of life
sing old songs and
new poems

artists rummage
in between
finding objects
to bang into stories

feet shuffle and stomp
high priced athletic shoes run
sandals stroll
high heels click on concrete

painters splash color on the street
daily calls to prayer

God's community
Muslim Jew Christian
Hebrew Buddhist Yoruba
cast holy shadows
on the trees

neighbors smile
at their images
reflected
in the windows
of wig shops
and the smell
of krispy kreme doughnuts
Jamaican food
fresh cooked collard greens

musicians play loudly
rehearsing the new

Black community
dances
the beginning

# Notes on the Black Freedom Struggle

Our struggle is for human rights, civil rights and self-determination. It is for human rights because it is part of the struggle for a just and humane world for all people. It is for civil rights because we are citizens of the country of our birth and choice and our rights as citizens must be respected, enforced and protected. It is for self-determination because Black people must have power to decide and determine their collective life including the relationship to other communities or institutional entities.

\* \* \*

Not one generation of Africans or their descendants African Americans believed that enslavement was their destiny. Every generation resisted slavery and every generation has resisted its aftermath racism, Jim Crow and 21st century violence and political and economic repression of Black people.

\* \* \*

Enslaved Africans and their descendants understood slavery as their condition not their destiny. They understood that to live, to survive the horrors of that great atrocity, was a victory. They knew they had to live to give birth to the next generation and the next generation until a generation was born free. They taught and held onto the vision. "If not me, my children. If not my children, their children. If not their children their children…but one day we will be free."

# Notes on Human Rights

At the core of every movement for justice is the issue of human rights. Too often our ideological, theological and political positions neglect the necessity to remember we are ultimately fighting for a just and humane world. In order to achieve that objective our struggles must align in purpose and program to move us toward greater understanding of and inclusion of all people.

\* \* \*

In the Black liberation struggle, we are experiencing challenging but important and required evolution in our thinking and practice. The emergence of Black Lives Matter as a force demanding justice for the Black community also forced us to confront traditional thinking and barriers within the African American community that obstructed the full participation of Black women in leadership of our movement. Black Lives Matter also forced us to deal with our biases and ignorance regarding our sisters and brothers in the LGBTQ community and the struggles they face within society and the Black community. Our struggle for justice must be for everyone, all people must be made whole by the results of the struggle for human rights. We are compelled to wrestle with our beliefs and ideas and develop a political movement and program that is committed to the human rights of all people. Black liberation practice must reflect that.

\* \* \*

December 2015, thousands of minor children from Honduras crossed the US border seeking refuge, some Americans throw rocks at them, curse them and demand their deportation back to Honduras. Imagine you lived in a place where your children are murdered, raped, kidnapped and turned into sex slaves. You live in soul crushing poverty. The government is corrupt and impotent so there is no protection against the criminals who have turned your town into a hellish prison. If you lived there you would probably do whatever you could to get your children to a safe place. Imagine as a parent, the agonizing decision to place your children in the hands of strangers who are paid to take them on a journey thousands of miles from home. Imagine the aching anxiety while you wait to know they are safe. Imagine they arrive safely in America and are confronted with the racism that lives on the border. It is a human rights issue and children from Honduras and other places where their lives are subjected to violence and poverty are refugees and should be welcomed and given the support they need. Not subjected to the hatefulness of American patriots.

* * *

During a recent winter it was so cold in Chicago they closed schools for a few days. I was watching the news and the announcer was smiling as he said Chicago's school children were going to be happy they were getting extra vacation days. My immediate thought was what about the children who need to get breakfast and lunch at school. How will they eat if school is closed? We live in a country that hides poverty and attacks the poor. Black impoverishment is growing and the policies of the current administration will not only increase poverty while reducing or eliminating the assistance low-income families need for basic necessities.

# Notes on Civil Rights

Before the defeat of slavery and the Confederacy and the passage of the 13th 14th and 15th Amendments, we were a people without legal status. We were not citizens, immigrants or refugees. After the overthrow of Reconstruction we were citizens without a country, a people denied our rights as citizens. During the Jim Crow era the laws of the US were subverted to prevent African American assertion of our rights as citizens. The mass movement of Black people forced the passage of the 1964 Civil Rights Bill and the 1965 Voting Rights as tools to enforce our civil rights. In the rhetoric of the racist right-wing of the 21st century there are echoes of the past. They want their country back, the way it was when Black people could be violated and denied their human and civil rights in the country of their birth and choice. We ain't going back.

\* \* \*

The Republican Party strategy to suppress the African American vote is an attempt to weaken political opposition to their policies and lessen the likelihood of electing Democratic or independent candidates to office. More importantly, it is essentially an attack on our right to be citizens by giving states the right to withhold the basic democratic right to vote. The act of voter suppression through the passage of laws and the enactment of barriers to greater Black voter participation is part of the long term strategy to delegitimize African American citizenship and weaken our political power. Again.

\* \* \*

Whatever our political assessment of President Obama, it is important to understand the birther movement led by Sarah Palin, Donald Trump and others was an attack on Black people and our right to be citizens of the US, the country of our birth or choice.

Republican claims that there is wide-spread voter fraud and Black people need to be watched and policed because we will cheat at the polls is not only false but contributes to the overall narrative of African Americans as not true Americans and criminals.

\* \* \*

Civil rights are the rights of citizens. The government is only legitimate if it protects and enforces the civil rights of all its citizens equally. Black people have in our recent consciousness the experience of living in a country where the government did not protect our rights or lives. We know the violence and abuse that occurs when racists local and state governments aligned with vigilantes have a federal government that is complicit by agreement or inaction. We understand the consequences of the growing power of the racist right-wing that under Trump is now in charge of the entire federal government.

\* \* \*

It is not a conversation on race that is needed to understand the great divide in the US. It is a conversation about citizenship and the different meaning it has for different groups. It is a conversation about a government that has facilitated the repression of Black people because the fundamental relationship that we have with this country is one of exploitation and disenfranchisement reinforced by violence. Even with the election of an African American president the relationship with the government did not improve. The systematic and sinister conspiracy of the Republican party to suppress Black voter, its determination to ramp up racist code words in the public discourse are all to remind the country that this is a white man's country and Black people are only here to serve their needs.

\* \* \*

All American citizens should be outraged that government agencies are attacking and murdering American citizens. We regularly criticize human and civil rights violations in other countries yet there is a general silence of political leadership in the white community on the increasing violence against American citizens. Thus the need for the conversation, are Black people and other people of color citizens in this country and if so, why is the government violating our citizenship rights to due process? Where is the proof that all citizens are treated equal and afforded equal protection under the law? There is no proof and African Americans understand that. it has long been known in the Black community. Now, with cell phones with cameras and social media it has become visible to the whole world. It has been made public and undeniable and yet there is still no outcry in the white community about government agencies attacking and murdering, illegally and unjustly incarcerating millions of US citizens.

\* \* \*

Despite advances in the economic position of many in the African American community, the needs of US capitalism require that Black people's resources remain vulnerable to be extracted for the benefit of others. It is a system that adapts, evolves, and adjusts in order to maintain the essential exploitative relationship formed in the slave trade and enslavement. Some of the ways this extraordinary exploitation occurs today include job discrimination, lower pay, higher interest rates, inadequate education, limited job opportunities, lack of access to services, taxation through tickets, fines and fees, the importation and distribution of drugs. The system adapts and creates new methods to enhance or replace old methods.

# Notes on Self-Determination

Our struggle is essentially a struggle for power. Power to live as free and whole human beings. Power to assert and protect our rights as citizens. And power to decide and enact our future as a people. Self-determination is the expression of that power and the manifestation of the idea of liberation or freedom.

\* \* \*

Since the 18th century self-determination has been a demand of African Americans. There has always been a consciousness that we must have power to determine our own future and to protect ourselves from those who want to oppress us. It has sometimes been expressed as Black Nationalism and the Black independence movement. It is evident in the Black church, HBCUs, Black sororities and fraternities. It is present in the Congressional Black Caucus and other political associations formed to protect and advocate for the interests of the Black community. It is visible in social justice movements, African American culture and education. It is a political need, a necessary power for any oppressed people to regain control over their lives, resources and relationship to the rest of the world. The demand for Black self-determination is necessary to center our movement for power to transform our communities. Human Rights, Civil Rights, Self-Determination!

\* \* \*

Coretta Scott King once said that if Martin and Malcolm had lived they would have grown closer and worked together for true liberation and self-determination.

# Notes on Black Lives Matter

In the second decade of the 21st century it is still necessary for African Americans to assert that Black Lives Matter. If we don't affirm it and assert it history tells us Black lives won't matter.

\* \* \*

The Black Lives Matter movement became the most important contemporary social justice movement in the US challenging the growing surge of state and vigilante violence against Black people.

\* \* \*

It gave form and leadership to an emerging mass resistance movement heavily populated with African American youth. Many of those young people now have several years of organizing experience working in communities throughout the US. Some have also sought and developed relationships with veteran organizers from the Civil Rights and Black Power movements connecting to a deep well of knowledge and experience to help build the new social justice movement.

\* \* \*

Perhaps the most important contribution of Black Lives Matter is its impact on the internal development of the Black community. As a movement initiated and led by Black women, some of whom are queer, BLM has forced us to confront the untenable patriarchal barriers that have persisted in denying women visible respected leadership and restricted participation of our historic movement. It has also forced us to address the vocal and unspoken bias against and marginalization of the LGBTQ members of our community. Ours is a struggle for human rights, civil rights and self-determination for all of us.

# TWO

NO ONE CAN BE AT PEACE UNLESS THEY HAVE FREEDOM

# Haiku for Peace

true warriors know
violence is not the way
even as they fight

# The United Front

Unity is built, constructed on common interests. In the struggle for Black liberation, the United Front has been and has to be a tool we commit to forge as a critical weapon. It is the most important tool to maximize the power of the Black community in pursuit of its demands.

* * *

United Fronts can be objective, subjective or both. They can be short term or long term and can be broad mass based or more narrowly focused on specific political objectives.

* * *

An objective United Front is where there is an alignment of interests and several forces, often from several communities, working toward a common goal. On a broad mass level, election campaigns are built on the principle of a united front. They mobilize diverse demographic, organizational and diverse groups to elect candidates, impact policy and legislation.

* * *

Unity is consistently called for within the African American community and struggle. It is often evoked as a needed behavior and force for positive development. Sometimes it is concretized in organized resistance to oppression. It is promoted as important in our family, local and national community. It cannot be talked into existence or hoped for. It must be built. Unity must be constructed around concrete objectives, guided by principles and within an organizational structure.

* * *

# Wrightsville, Georgia

In the early 1980s, I was doing voting rights, anti-klan and justice work in Wrightsville GA with the local Black community and the New Justice Movement, National Black United Front, SCLC and other activists. The Black people of Wrightsville were under siege by a system left over from slavery and Jim Crow, a racist confederate sheriff and the KKK. Demonstrations and mass meetings to support voter education and registration were being conducted weekly. A young man active in the movement had been shot while traveling home one night from a community meeting. The demonstrations were being observed by the Justice Department, State Troopers and the Georgia Bureau of Investigation. During one scorching hot Georgia day, as the brave local Black people and over a thousand supporters from all across the US, marched toward the town square, a local white man sat fuming in his pickup truck on a dirt road that intersected the road we were marching down. He was visibly agitated because he had to wait for the wave of Black people and their allies to pass before he could go forward. He became so enraged that he backed his truck up about 75 yards and sat there revving the engine like he was going to lurch forward at any moment. A sister and brother who were members of our security team were in the intersection to protect the marchers and had turned to face the truck which seemed to further anger the white man in his pick-up. A Black GBI agent who had been in Wrightsville for several months and had been at most of the demonstrations was also on that side of the march and saw the stand-off happening and escalating rapidly. Just as he stepped between our security and the truck, the driver floored the pedal and came flying toward the intersection with the intention to drive his truck into the demonstrators. The GBI agent drew his weapon and aimed it at the driver, our security people turned to move people out of the path of the truck and the violence the driver was clearly ready to commit against us. The GBI agent stood in the middle of the road and aimed directly at the head of the driver. Seconds flew by as we scrambled to get people out of the way. The agent remained planted, weapon ready, the driver in his sights as he came speeding forward. All of this happened in just a few seconds and we braced for the crash and the gunfire that was certain from the agent and our security who were there protecting the people. The driver must have decided to live because he suddenly slammed on his brakes, skidding to a halt less than a yard from the agent. As soon as the truck came to a stop the agent, with his gun still on the driver, snatched open the door, grabbed him by the neck and threw him to the ground where he cuffed and arrested him. I asked the agent about the incident later. He said, "I was doing my job as a GBI agent and as a Black man I couldn't live with myself if I'd allowed him to continue." It was a lesson in the nature of united front. Where interests converge we unite, if only for a moment, if it will benefit the people.

# Remembering Reverend Gerard Jean-Juste
February 7, 1946 – May 27, 2009

I've met many people with the title Christian minister, but very few seemed to live up to it. The Haitian leader Reverend Gerard Jean-Juste was a Catholic priest and one of those few true ministers I've been fortunate to meet on my own complicated spiritual journey. I had not seen him in many years but news of his death invaded my consciousness causing days of mourning, weeks and months of thinking about him and even today almost a decade later, I am impacted by the life he lived serving the people of Haiti, championing their humanity and human rights, ministering to their needs. This is a notice I sent out after hearing of his death.

Dear Family,

It is with great regret that I write to tell you that Father Gerard Jean-Juste, one of the most remarkable people I've ever met, made his transition on May 27. I first met Father Jean-Juste in the early 1980's when he was director of the Haitian Refugee Center in Miami. A group of us brought him to Atlanta to build support for his work and we also collected several truckloads of clothes to donate to the refugee community he was serving. Father Jean-Juste preached and practiced liberation theology and spent his life fighting for the rights of his people and all people. He was fearless and compassionate, humorous and scholarly, kind and gentle with the confidence and will of those who know they have chosen to be on the right side of history. Father Jean-Juste had been imprisoned in Haiti for his opposition to the corruption and oppression of the government. Designated a prisoner of conscience by Amnesty International a broad international coalition fought for and eventually won his release. He was one of the few true ministers I've met on my own life journey, always ministering to the least of these, always fighting for the rights of the dispossessed, always feeding the hungry, visiting those imprisoned, loving the unloved. If you get a minute, take note of a life well lived in service to others and the God he believed in. Long live the spirit of Father Gerard Jean-Juste!!!

\* \* \*

Although some feel we no longer need Black History Month, it remains important to have a focused period of acknowledgment and recognition to remind us that Negro History Week created in 1926 by the great African American historian Carter G Woodson and later expanded to Black History Month were/are acts of resistance and self-determination. It continues to have importance as a tool of education and affirmation in many academic and non-academic spaces including communities, faith institutions, public schools, civic and social organizations. Movements to honor and teach the story of Black people year-round, and include native peoples, Hispanics, Asians and other people in the telling is critical to US and world history. Maintaining the February focus is an important connection to our historic struggle and the future we envision. It is comparable to holidays that make us pause, reflect, remember and renew.

# Notes on Electoral Politics

No one gave Black people the right to vote. We paid for it with the pain and blood, the lives and deaths of thousands of our courageous ancestors who needed, wanted and fought for the right to decide their own destiny. They wanted the right to be full citizens of the country of their birth and the rights that come with citizenship. They wanted the political power that would help them access and develop resources to improve the conditions of their lives. They wanted government that represented them and their interests. They fought for the right to be heard and represented by their peers on juries, in local government, state legislators and the three branches of federal government. They also knew it was just one tool in the fight for liberation.

\* \* \*

In the 100 years between the defeat of the criminal confederacy (1865) and the Voting Rights Act (1965) the citizenship rights guaranteed by the Constitution of the United States were openly violated by the Jim Crow laws and terrorism of southern governments and vigilantes like the KKK. They were also severely restricted by the economic violence and police repression of the racist northern governments. In both cases it was done with the complicity of the federal government including Congress, Federal Courts and every president that occupied the White House. The mass movement of Black people organized for civil rights and Black power in local and national organizations and united fronts, and with the support of their allies, dismantled the Jim Crow terroristic governments and brought major changes to the north and the west. Too often I hear Black people say nothing has changed. That is clearly not true and represents a cynical view of our history here and dishonors the struggle and sacrifices of those who came before us. Each generation moves us forward, sometimes inches, sometimes miles. It is movement forced by a movement.

\* \* \*

Remember Selma! 2015 50 years ago a bridge was crossed a battle won a victory claimed in a long war that spanned centuries. We take this moment to honor those working women and men whose courage, strength and faith reminded us that the people are more powerful than those who choose to violently attempt to oppress and exploit us. But current events also remind us, this war is not over, there are more bridges to cross and more battles to fight and that we too must have courage, must stay strong and have faith in the power of our people to defeat those who seek to deny our humanity and justice.

\* \* \*

Too often, we who consider ourselves radical or revolutionary, refuse to participate in electoral politics or spend a considerable amount of energy hurling insults from the sidelines at candidates or elected officials whom we deem sell-outs for a variety of reasons, some legitimate, most an indication of our own political immaturity. We mistakenly withdraw from a process that can mobilize and empower the people to take act collectively. Electoral campaigns are inherently united fronts that pull people with differences into a process and organizational thrust around common interests. It is mass education, recruitment of and development of new activists, building of local political structures and the transfer of power into the hands of the people. Electoral politics must result in a transference of power into the hands of the people so that there is access to the resources that they need to positively affect their lives. This is not a static process, for every victory there is a push back from those we've wrested power from. Building and sustaining local community based, mass organizations is essential to the fight to gain and consolidate political power for the people.

\* \* \*

Two recent successful mayoral campaigns demonstrate the use of and importance of community based, progressive Black electoral politics. Both come out of the Black Power tradition, one in the Black belt south and the other in the Black urban north. Both built community based organizations and made alliances with progressive forces throughout the city. In Jackson Mississippi the 2013 election of Chokwe Lumumba was the culmination of decades of struggle to empower Black people in the south through advocating for Black self-determination and nationhood. In Newark, NJ Ras Baraka was elected as a result of another long struggle for Black community empowerment that began with the Black Nationalist led united front to elect the first African American Mayor Ken Gibson in 1970. Mayor Baraka had worked in community empowerment organizations, taught and been a principal in the public school system, been elected to city council from the South Ward. He is the son of artists/activists Amiri and Amina Baraka and was elected May 13, 2014 just months after his father's death in January that year.

\* \* \*

Resistance is constant. Change is incremental. Revolution is structural transformation of a political and economic system so there is redistribution of the resources of society and the machinery of governing in the hands of people. Each requires greater organizational capacity.

\* \* \*

Mass demonstrations, political organizations, voter education and registration, building independent Black institutions including schools, civic organizations, businesses, faith centers and self-defense organizations were and are all part of developing capacity to advance and protect the interests of Black people.

\* \* \*

Those who seek to continue to oppress and exploit us engage in all kinds of nefarious activities to make sure we either can't vote or don't vote. They understand the potential power our collective political will has. The national African American vote is responsible for the election of the past five Democratic presidents. John Kennedy ('60), Lyndon Johnson ('64), Jimmy

Carter ('76), Bill Clinton ('92) and Barack Obama ('08) won because of the almost universal and unified national vote of the Black community. Hillary Clinton lost the 2016 election but 88% of Black people voted for her. The Democratic Party coalition cannot win a presidential election without the Black vote. What do we as a national community want and need for our vote? We need a local and national process to develop a national agenda and organization to fight for that agenda. The organization must be grounded in local political education and training and a community based process for vetting, selecting and holding accountable those who get our vote. What are we willing to do if our needs are not met?

# Notes on Self-Defense against Racist Terrorism

Human beings have the right to defend themselves against those who seek to harm them or their families. US citizens also have that right.

* * *

The criminals who had purchased kidnapped Africans and were transporting them in the ship called the Amistad to be sold as slaves in America were overthrown in the most famous uprising on a slave ship. The case of those heroic Africans went all the way to the US Supreme Court where their lawyer, the former president of the US John Quincy Adams, successfully argued that they had the human right to defend themselves against kidnappers, murderers and slave traders. Although the Amistad case was won and the defendants were allowed to return to their home in Africa, the right of self-defense for Black people has always been problematic for those who exploited and oppressed us. The plantocracy, white supremacists vigilantes and racist local, state and federal government have been or are explicitly or implicitly against Black self-defense.

* * *

Frederick Douglass encouraged Black people to join the Union Army for two reasons. To get guns and training to fight for freedom. To have guns and training to keep their freedom.

* * *

Robert F. Williams and Mable Williams are important leaders of the Civil Rights and Black Power movement who advocated and organized armed self-defense for a Black community under siege in Monroe North Carolina. Their story is not taught but every generation needs to know the self-defense component of the Black liberation movement. Robert and Mable Williams, the Deacons for Defense and Justice and many other organized self-defense resistance activists and movements are part of the history of our struggle. Read Williams' *Negroes with Guns*; *We Will Shoot Back* by Akinyele Umoja; and *Radio Free Dixie* by Timothy Tyson. There's also a good documentary on the Monroe struggle, *Negroes with Guns: Rob Williams and Black Power.*

# Politics of the African American Community: Lessons from the 2014 Midterm Elections

Republicans and Democrats both ran anti-Obama campaigns in the 2014 midterms. The Republicans won and the Democrats lost.

As an important demographic in key areas of the country African Americans are capable of influencing or determining the outcome of elections in major cities and several states. This importance is clear to the Democratic and Republican parties who both have a history of actively soliciting or attempting to suppress the African American vote. This ebb and flow of the relationship between the Black community and the two parties dates back to Reconstruction and continues to this day.

We experienced evidence of this in the 2014 midterm elections as Republicans actively engaged in attempts to suppress and limit the African American vote in key states. We also experienced desperate Democrats pleading for the embrace of the African American community as a last hope for key senatorial and state elections.

In the case of the Republicans this is a part of an overall strategy to appeal to white voters and neutralize a key Democratic constituency. Reducing the influence of African Americans helped Republicans capture both houses of Congress and hold onto key governorships and state legislatures. The Democrats have become adept at presenting themselves as the party willing to stand up for African American rights and interests. However, in the face of the Republican attacks on voting rights and the first African American president, the Democratic Party's tepid response leaves the Black community wanting in American politics.

The attack on Black voter rights is essentially an attempt to deny citizenship. Full citizenship for blacks has been the core of the issue of the Civil Rights struggle since the Dred Scott 1857 Supreme Court ruling that blacks cannot be citizens and therefore have no rights. 2014 marks the 50th anniversary of the 1964 Civil Rights Act and 2015 is the 50th anniversary of the Voting Rights Act. Both of them were necessary remedies to the denial through law and custom of Black citizenship. Yet even as we acknowledge those landmarks, Black voter suppression remains in American political culture an effective strategy to win elections.

Whether we agree or disagree with President Obama, the vast majority of African Americans believe he has been widely disrespected. He has been obstructed by Republicans who are determined to insure his failure and in the 2014 midterm election we witnessed the more subtle disrespect of President Obama by Democrats. They unwisely treated him as a pariah, keeping him from key campaigns. This strategy suggested that Democrats agreed with Republicans that President Obama's administration was a failure, despite facts that prove otherwise. In addition to having passed the Affordable Care Act, brought the country back from the brink of economic disaster and significantly reduced unemployment, under President Obama more than 5 million jobs have been created compared to President Bush at fewer than 2 million. While there have been tremendous challenges, there have also been important successes. Yet the Democratic Party chose not to run on its actual record, instead they ran a softer anti-Obama campaign. They seemed convinced that Black people either would not or could not understand what they were doing and why they were doing it and therefore would still go to the polls in numbers high enough to deliver a Democratic victory. The anti-Black Obama strategy worked for the Republicans and failed for the Democrats who were both trying to win white voters (especially in the South) who have been misled into believing that the election of Black President Obama is an evil that must be corrected.

Now in the aftermath of the midterms blacks have to make choices. Do we continue to play the game of blind allegiance to Democrats? Do we run to the Republicans who are openly hostile to blacks, women and Hispanics? Or do we organize ourselves into an independent political force, win local elections and influence national elections to insure the interests of the African American community is served instead of just being served up by those who continue to disrespect and disappoint us.

*Originally published in the Atlanta Voice Newspaper November 24, 2014*

# From the Cracks in the Sidewalk

From the cracks in the sidewalk
I see the flowers grow

I hear that music flying
sweet from an open window

Watch little brown children laugh
at their own dancing feet

With food from our garden sit
with our neighbors to eat

# Mothers' Day

I attended my mother's graduation from the University of Detroit when I was 9. She wanted to be a teacher. She was one of 5 daughters of parents who made their living as a domestic worker and a janitor (and sometime card dealer in the gambling clubs). We went to school with her when she had to attend class and there was no aunt, grandparent or neighbor to keep us, and my father was at one of his 2 or 3 jobs. My brother and I would walk the 2.5 miles to campus with her and sit in the hall outside her classroom with books, crayons, paper and puzzles. She started teaching at 31 and worked as an activist educator for 50 years. I was a full time Black liberation movement activist poet and cultural worker out of high school and worked in auto factories and in the labor movement. At 44 I told my mother I was thinking of going to school but there was some hesitation because I'd be almost 50 when I finished. She smiled at me and gently asked the scholarly question, "How old will you be if you don't go to school?" We laughed about that for years. At both of my graduations she was there smiling when I received my BA and PhD and each time she asked sarcastically, "How old is you now?"

\* \* \*

Happy Mother's Day to all the women who raised and raise us and fight against those who would crush our dreams!

# Remembering Our Mother
Mama Imani Humphrey (March 8, 1932 – March 8, 2016

With two daughters and two sons and 2 grandchildren sitting with her holding her hands, our beloved mother Mama Imani Humphrey made her transition to ancestor today, 84 years from the day she was born March 8, 1932. She was an influential Detroit activist-educator who taught in Detroit Public Schools, at Wayne County Community College and Wayne State University before founding two independent African centered schools. A leading scholar for over 40 years, she focused on the education of African American children and in training a new generation of educators. Founder of Aisha Shule and the W.E.B. DuBois Academy she was a master teacher of students and a master mentor of teachers. Over the course of her career as an educator she directly taught thousands of students and trained hundreds of teachers and indirectly impacted thousands more.

The third of five sisters, she graduated from Inkster High School, University of Detroit and Wayne State University. A poet and Black art historian she was our family's last elder from her generation and she actively guided her 4 children, 14 grandchildren, 14 great grandchildren, dozens of nieces, nephews and countless daughters and sons who joined our extended family. Hers, a life well lived as a servant of our people who affectionately called her Mama Imani. Her life a testament to the importance of teachers.

# Lunch with My Father

From my father and grandfathers I learned there are men who are fathers, by blood or choice, and have upheld the unspoken code: under no circumstances do we abandon our children.

* * *

My father, Richard Humphrey Jr., worked long hours as a community organizer who advocated for African American youth in Detroit. Occasionally, he'd sign me out of school to spend the afternoon together. He'd take me to a local lounge (in Detroit that's what bars were called) and we'd eat fried fish sandwiches, shoot pool and talk. After lunch I'd ride with him to meetings or some community event he thought would be interesting for me. I thought it was just hanging with my father and it wasn't until later in my adult life that I realized how much he was educating me about the life of Black people in the most distressed neighborhoods in Detroit and how we had to be organized to make change.

* * *

During the fall semester in 1969, my junior year at Mumford HS, I was summoned to the office. It wasn't unusual because I was frequently there for breaking various rules as a result of organizing Black students. That time my father was standing there and his presence alarmed me because my instinct was to prepare to receive some kind of tragic news about my family. Fortunately, that was not the case. He had come to get me because one of the leaders of the Black liberation movement was flying into Detroit, returning from exile abroad. He was pulling me out of school so I could attend the press conference and meet Robert F. Williams, a heroic figure in the Civil Rights/Black Power movement. With his wife and life partner Mable, he had organized the Black community in Monroe, North Carolina to defend themselves with arms against the persistent violent attacks of the KKK. After being falsely accused of kidnapping an elderly white couple during an intense period of confrontation with racist terrorists and under threat of assassination, Robert and Mable Williams with their children went into exile in Cuba, China and Africa. There are many sources to learn about this hidden story of the Civil Rights Movement, including Williams' book Negroes with Guns, Timothy Tyson's Radio Free Dixie and the documentary film Negroes with Guns: Rob Williams and Black Power.

With many others my father and I welcomed Rob back to the states. He and Mable with their sons moved to Baldwin Michigan where he joined the local NAACP and continued working on behalf of his local community while also lecturing and writing about the African American liberation struggle.

\* \* \*

Robert F. Williams faced charges in North Carolina and in 1975 after years of legal negotiations he was finally going back to face and resolve the fraudulent case against him. Amiri Baraka, who had spent time with Rob in Cuba and who was the national chair of the Congress of African People (CAP) sent two of our NewArk based members, Jalia and Tarik to Detroit to accompany the Williams' to NC. As a member of the CAP Central Committee and the Detroit Chair, I was charged with organizing the press conference at Detroit Metropolitan Airport before his departure. Local, national and international media packed the room to hear from one of the most influential leaders of the Black Liberation Movement. After introducing him and observing the interaction with the reporters, I remembered the last time I'd been at a press conference for Robert F. Williams. It was the day my father checked me out of school to witness his return from exile.

\* \* \*

As an adult, I continued the tradition of unplanned lunches with my father. I'd occasionally stop by his Comprehensive Youth Services Program office on Mack Avenue on Detroit's east side and see if he could break away for an hour. As was our practice, we'd go to one of his favorite lounges for fried fish sandwiches. During one of those lunches Marvin Gaye walked in to the lounge, spoke to everyone and sat down at the piano. There was a moment of anticipation but no attempt by any of the patrons or staff to interrupt or interfere in whatever Marvin was getting ready to do. He sat there for a few minutes with his eyes closed and then slowly placed his hands on the piano keys, opened his eyes and started playing. He had walked into the lounge as if he was driving his car and something compelled him to stop and find a piano immediately. He flowed between blues and jazz, classical and Broadway show tunes. It was as if he had just opened up a huge reservoir of music inside his head and let it pour out however it came. We ate, listened and talked quietly. So did everyone else. Nobody moved until Marvin finished a couple of hours later. My father and I were both late going back to work.

\* \* \*

There is no way to quantify how much I learned from my father and how much his love and support meant to me. I am eternally grateful for everyday he walked this earth with me. Happy Father's Day to all the men who walk with their children.

\* \* \*

To all the men who are or were fathers in their practice of life in spite of our pain, our shortcomings, our confusion, our doubt, our fatigue, our rage, our insecurities, our depression, our wounds and every other obstacle, give your best to love and parent our children so they may not only survive but grow strong enough to give their contribution to making this a just and humane world, thank you.

# Remembering Muhammad Ali

On the morning of April 28, 1967 Muhammad Ali was the Heavyweight Champion of the World. By that afternoon he had refused induction into the US military as a conscientious objector, refusing to fight for a country that oppressed his people at home and other people of color abroad. He was charged as a draft dodger and became the most important symbol of the widening resistance to the US war in Viet Nam. Immediately, a white backlash sought to strip him of his title, prevent him from earning a living at his trade and lock him up in prison. Ali was not afraid. He had been mentored by Malcolm X, was a member of the Nation of Islam and supported the mass movement of Black people for freedom, justice and equality. He didn't bend or ask white people to forgive him. He didn't back step. He pushed forward, fighting the case in court and prepared to go to prison if he had to. He was our hero.

On June 4, 1967 Muhammad Ali met with a group of professional Black athletes in Cleveland at what is known as the Ali Summit. Amongst those attending were three of the most famous and influential African American athletes in the world, Jim Brown, Bill Russell and Lew Alcindor who later changed his name to Kareem Abdul Jabbar. The purpose of the meeting was to discuss Ali's decision to make a stand for Black people against the war and for those in attendance to decide if they would support him. After a closed door meeting, Ali, Brown, Russell, Alcindor and the others held a press conference where they stood with Ali and supported his action against the war. It was a profound statement of Black unity, a testament to Ali's fearlessness outside of the ring and the courage of the other Black men at the summit.

On June 15 1967 Muhammad Ali fought an exhibition fight for charity at Detroit's Cobo Arena. Some Detroit papers describe the crowd as a disappointing 3000 or so in attendance. The Black press reported more than 7000. My brother Chris, my cousin Stevie and I were taken to see the great Muhammad Ali by my father and Stevie's dad, Uncle Ted. After watching the exhibition and marveling at the speed and precision of the champ we were told to sit and wait while the arena emptied out after the event. The three of us boys were restless and bored sitting in the empty space waiting for the two men to return and take us to eat and home. After about 30 minutes they emerged from behind a curtain and with them was Muhammad Ali. He walked right up to us saying, "Hey guys, I'm Muhammad Ali." My brother said, "We know who you are, Champ." He then reached behind Stevie's ear and pulled out a quarter. For the next 20 minutes he stood with us in the empty arena, did magic tricks and talked to us about being proud of who we are and doing good in school and doing something for our community.

On June 20 Muhammad Ali was convicted of draft evasion and sentenced to 5 years in prison, a 3 year ban from boxing and a $10,000 fine. He didn't' bend, ask for forgiveness or back step. He pushed forward even as they stripped him of his titles and license to fight. His courage inspired us. Government persecution of him was added to a long list of grievances piled up high and as a weight to crush the spirit of the Black revolution.

July 23, 1967 the Detroit rebellion erupted in the most ferocious and deadliest revolt of the 1960s. My father was a community organizer working in the neighborhood where the rebellion started. He left our home to go into the center of the rebellion to organize and provide relief and assistance to those who needed it. It was dangerous work and he explained it later as necessary for Black men to stand-up and do what needed to be done. Like Ali, he added.

# Graduations in the Black Community
May 21, 2016

Last night our amazing creative son Malik graduated from Westlake HS. And as we sat in a sea of a three thousand Black people from 400 families we shared a moment of affirmation of our collective story always moving forward. We cheered and laughed and celebrated another generation making strides despite the barriers. We sat there together, his mother and father, his sisters and brother, three aunts, two uncles, four cousins and his grandmother who drove over from Grenada Mississippi. Sitting with that inspired mass of families and the ancient hope of our children having good lives, we felt our strength and knew our power. For 3 hours we existed in our peace and dreams and joy and there was nothing there to violate or commit violence against us. And it was beautiful and there was love and there was light.

# Remembering Chokwe Lumumba
August 2, 1947 – February 25, February 14

I drove from Atlanta to Jackson Mississippi on Friday Feb 21 2014 to meet with my brother Chokwe Lumumba. On the way there I thought a lot about the influence of Malcolm X (it was the anniversary of his assassination) and Chokwe whom I first met while in high school with his sisters, in Detroit 1968-71. As the years passed in the sped up time of the liberation movement we worked in different liberation organizations, he in the Provisional Government of the Republic of New Africa and I in the Congress of African People. Sometimes we went years without seeing each other, but the bond of brotherhood forged in struggle remained strong. Since his election we'd communicated with short texts and that visit was the first time I'd see him as the Mayor. A good part of the afternoon was spent in a wide ranging discussing about our families, the importance of his election and vision for Jackson and the necessity to build support for the Jackson project nationally. I sat with him and grew more inspired each minute because I realized that after 46 years knowing this brother, this fierce fighter for the people, this brilliant advocate for justice, this sonbrotherhusband-father, this highly respected and often honored leader, his laughter and smile, his kindness and caring, his genuine love for his work as a servant was exactly the same as when he came to show support for us, high school students who'd been attacked by the police because we had the audacity to demand quality education that included our history and literature. I remember how he stood up for us and our cause. His greatness was evident then and his light never dimmed. Not even now. Not ever.

# Black History: A Legacy of Resistance and Assertion

Black History Month 2016 occurs in the midst of a White supremacy, right-wing uprising against the African American community and people of color. This uprising is countrywide and includes the constant violence of the state including police killings of Black people and the poisoning of a Black majority city. It also includes the rise in vigilante attacks, the assault on voting rights and the disenfranchisement of Black communities through state takeovers of local governments. It is the erasure of the great atrocity of slavery from public education and countless other attempts to suppress the progress and power of Black people. Under the banner of "taking our country back" or "making America great again" and other coded phrases, this uprising is propagated by public officials, public personalities and private organizations. It is an attempt to stop the future in the same way the antebellum south sent hundreds of thousands to die in the Civil War to delay the end of slavery.

The African American local and national community response to this contemporary violent uprising has been the eruption of Black protests, organizing and struggle seen in cities and on college campuses across the United States. As a response came the emergence of Black Lives Matter and other movements and the reinvigoration of veteran organizations and activists. It is also stirred a new generation to take their place on the front lines of our long struggle for freedom.

Black history and culture have a legacy of resistance and assertion. We have always resisted our oppression and asserted our humanity. Not one generation of enslaved Black people in the United States believed slavery was their destiny. It was understood as a condition that would be ended one day. Each generation passed on the knowing, "If not me, my children. If not my children, their children. If not their children, then their children… but one day we will be free." It sustained us, kept us alive and moving forward for three and a half centuries. Contrary to the lies that have been told, it was never a passive idea in our community. It was always understood that freedom had to be fought for and won. Oppression had to be resisted and our humanity had to be asserted by our own dignity, our own struggle and commitment to live as free human beings.

This is the legacy bequeathed by every generation that preceded us. It is from that legacy that we draw our strength, our resilience, our courage and commitment to fight. It is from that legacy that the great historian Dr. Carter G. Woodson led the establishment of Negro History Week in 1926 (officially becoming Black History Month in 1976) to resist the denial of Black contribution to the world and to assert our genius. Black history is a history of resistance and assertion.

"We are going back to that beautiful history and it is going to inspire us to greater achievements." Dr. Carter G. Woodson

*Originally published February 6, 2016 in Rolling Out Magazine*

# Notes on Violence in the Black Community

We have to (and only we can) end violence in our families. No exemptions. No excuses. Exemptions and excuses are justifications subject to interpretation. We continue to debate the acceptable level of violence against children and women and men. There is no acceptable level.

\* \* \*

Socio-economic explanations for violence are not a sufficient response we need solutions that transform communities into safe liberated zones of development.

\* \* \*

Recently re-read *"Tell no lies, Claim no easy victories"* by the great African revolutionary Amilcar Cabral. He wrote, "Always bear in mind that the people are not fighting for ideas, for the things in anyone's head. They are fighting to win material benefits, to live better and in peace, to see their lives go forward, to guarantee the future of their children." It made me think about what had been achieved in Jackson, Mississippi with the election of Chokwe Lumumba as mayor of Jackson Mississippi. While visiting with him I said, "You've spent your career fighting police and now you have to run a police department." He responded, "I know, ain't that something." We laughed at the irony. The reality was he'd been thinking of and advocating changes in policing for years. Chokwe and the organizations he belonged to were respected in the community because of the practical solutions they sought for the problems of the people. The election was not symbolic, they are building people's democracy to transfer power to the people, to address their needs and transform how the city was governed. Public safety was one of his administrations major priorities. It is an example for our movement.

# Notes on Winter Holidays

Thanksgiving Thoughts – When we gather today with our families let us give thanks for the food to nourish our bodies to keep us strong in this struggle for justice and peace. Give thanks for the strength that comes from the love of our families, those close, extended and ancestral so we are reminded of our capacity to not only resist but to defeat those who seek to deny us a just and humane world. When we gather today let us give thanks and commit to give more than thanks in whatever way we can.

\* \* \*

Today a moment to reflect and share on the gifts of life and in life we are thankful for. A pause to remember a unique moment in the history of this country when First Nations peoples shared their spiritual knowledge of and relationship to nature so that strangers could survive and know that we have a responsibility to take care of the earth and in doing so will be blessed with its bounty. I wish all of us sacred moments of generosity.

\* \* \*

December 25
Today reminds us that any child, every child, regardless of the circumstances of their birth has the potential to change the world.

\* \* \*

Kwanzaa remains an important reminder of ancestral connection and the power of the Black liberation movement to resist white supremacy and redefine the culture of the African American community. In the Congress of African People we joined with others in the Black Liberation Movement and built Kwanzaa from a holiday practiced by a few hundred people to hundreds of thousands and eventually millions. There was no social media or email. We went family by family, church by church, school by school, community by community teaching the principles, Umoja-Unity, Kujich-agulia-Self Determination, Ujima-Collective Work and Responsibility, Uja-maa-Cooperative Economics, Nia-Purpose, Kuumba-Creativity and Imani-Faith. We held small and large community gatherings teaching the symbols and rituals. We discussed it in Black media, radio and papers. We connected it to the work we were doing in communities around education, housing, social justice and political empowerment. It was a gathering, for family for community. It was an organizing tool and a call for unity. Today, it is waning in popularity and practice, but we shouldn't allow it. We are losing connection to those cultural bridges that brought us over and that we need to insure the next generation doesn't forget.

# Notes on War

I watch the faces and hear the sounds. On television. The digitized images and words fly across the world to tell us something horrible is happening to some people somewhere where violence is thrown at them in explosions of hatred and greed hurtling through narrow streets and wide open wilderness of desert or forest. Cities bombed, villages burned, burial grounds for thousands, sometimes millions. The people, sometimes urban sometimes rural seemingly far beyond the reality we live until our own young return from their tours with broken bodies and shattered minds to remind us that there is a cost and eventually in the much celebrated globalization, everyone must pay. Sometimes the sound is so close we call our relatives living there to find out what is really going on or to tell them we are alright. I hear the noise and see the faces and most of all I hear the commentary of children in places of extreme violence, in war zones, telling their stories and singing their songs. I've heard the voices of children.

# No Lies About War

My students have asked about my position on war. I am against war. I'm anti-war. I am also against us acting like our daughters and sons, brothers and sisters are not currently in war. In the US we should demand that the front page or lead story of every news outlet everyday report on the killed, wounded, psychologically damaged soldiers and devastated families to remind us of the real cost of war. Perhaps then we will not glorify the actions of politicians and corporate profiteers when they drive the country into war.

# The Death of War

It is not the blood
Animals will lick it clean

It is not the flesh
Insects will devour it too

It is not the tears
Fauna will grow from it soon

It is not the darkness
or the noise
or the shattering and
breaking of things

It is not the flowing blood
It is not the wounded flesh
It is not the draining tears

It is not the darkness
or the noise
or the shattering and
breaking of things

It is not orphaned children
or women raped

It is not the drying blood
It is not the rotting flesh
It is not the staining tears

It is not the darkness
or the noise
or the shattering and
breaking of things

It is not limbs torn away
or men gone mad

It is not the crusty blood
It is not the burned flesh
It is not the shaming tears

It is not the darkness
or the noise
or the shattering and
breaking of things

It is only us and them
It is only you and me

It is my blood and your blood
It is my flesh and your flesh
It is my tears and your tears

It is our blood and theirs
It is our flesh and theirs
It is our tears and theirs

It is our children
And our women
And our men

For them we must sing
The death of war
For them we must bring
The death of war

# THREE

NO ONE CAN BE AT PEACE UNLESS THEY HAVE FREEDOM

# Blue Black (For Radcliff Bailey)

You noticed

the world
began
with Black paint
spilling
across the planet

the night was born
in smoke and sounds
cracking silence
into 8th notes

You heard

music
formed the oceans
trees sang language

sun flashed
for photos
of ancestors
dancing in fire

lightning spotlights
rhythm born
under moon beats

You remembered

a Black star
sailing east down
highways
with wings

our children
flying

# Haki Madhubuti, Third World Press, and the Legacy of the Black Arts Movement

My first novel, *In the Shadow of the Son*, was published by Third World Press in 1998. Before that it was a file on my computer and I'd had some conversations with a few major corporate publishing houses who had expressed interest. They all said the same thing and asked the same questions. "We love the story and writing but..." Their hesitation was always the result of something about the politics or the Black characters who seemed unfamiliar to them, or the lack of white people in the book, or the poetry that they didn't understand and on and on. I understood what their questions and statements really meant. They did not feel I was writing for them and wanted me to make changes to make it a different book, addressed to a different audience.

They were right, I was not writing for or to them. I always write to speak from and to Black people in the same way Russian writers speak to and from Russians, or French writers, or Chinese writers or any writer who writes from their own historical or cultural experience. Like other writers I expect readers to enter our world through our stories and access them as a human being listening with an open heart and mind to the experience of another human being. I refused to change my novel and so it sat as a file in my computer in Atlanta, memorialized by a desk drawer full of rejection letters. There was also a printed copy I'd mailed to my mother in Detroit who after reading it, sat it somewhere in her house. I assumed it was sitting in Detroit.

Unbeknownst to me, she mailed it to Haki Madhubuti in Chicago. A couple of weeks later, Haki called me and said, "We're going to publish your novel." It wasn't a question or negotiation. It was an affirmation, a way of saying there is a place, a home for writers like you and work like yours. And that place is here amongst the Black giants and the poets, the truth tellers, the thinkers and doers. With that phone call, my name was added to the list of Black writers published by Third World Press. I was grateful to be drummed into the TWP family, to be part of the legacy it fostered and of course to get my novel into the hands of readers.

For fifty years (1967-2017) Third World Press has published some of our most dynamic voices and books that would have remained unpublished manuscripts in the desk drawers of many important writers. As noted on their website, TWP writers include poet and publisher, Dudley Randall; Illinois Poet Laureate and Pulitzer Prize winner, Gwendolyn Brooks; poets Amiri Baraka, Sonia Sanchez, Mari Evans, Margaret Walker, Gil Scott Heron, Sterling Plumpp and Haki R. Madhubuti; world-renown psychiatrists Frances Cress Welsing and Carl C. Bell; editor Hoyt W. Fuller; historians John Henrik Clarke, Jacob Carruthers and Chancellor Williams; playwright and producer Woody King, Jr.; writers Herb Boyd, Useni Eugene Perkins, Ayi Kwei Armah, Kalamu ya Salaam, Pearl Cleage and South African Poet Laureate Keorapetse Kgositsile; actors and playwrights Ossie Davis and Ruby Dee; artists Murry DePillars, Calvin Jones, and Jon Lockard; authors Nathan Hare, Asa G. Hilliard III, Derrick Bell, Barbara A. Sizemore, Geneva Smitherman, Lita Hooper, Diane Turner, Julianne Malveaux, Bakari Kitwana, Marc Lamont Hill, Thabiti Lewis, Mumia Abu Jamal, Kelly Norman Ellis, Tony Medina and others.

Haki Madhubuti is one of our major poets and essayists and a principal architect of the Black Arts Movement. He is a prolific writer, lecturer, scholar, educator and institution builder. He founded TWP in 1967 to publish Black poets and writers. It was one of the hundreds of independent institutions created during the Black Arts Movement that included journals, theater companies, publishing houses and dance companies, galleries and artists collectives. Most did not last into the 21st century. There are only a few theater and dance companies and a couple of publications and galleries from the era. Of the publishing companies, TWP is the only one that has never stopped publishing or gone out of business. It is now the oldest continuously publishing Black independent press in the history of the US. It has survived because of the commitment to Black self-determination, the leadership of Haki Madhubuti and the will of past and present employees and volunteers who have often labored under difficult and stressful conditions to insure Black voices are heard. TWP is an enduring example of why independent Black institutions are critical to the advancement of our interests and our power. Without TWP, gaping holes would exist in our intellectual and literary history.

The Black Arts Movement left an expansive multi-discipline artistic and activist legacy. Fortunately, there is growing scholarship on its history, artists, institutions and enduring influence. It is imperative that the new group of Black scholars study and write about the contribution, impact and importance of the work of Haki Madhubuti and the story of Third World Press in the struggle for Black liberation and self-determination. It is also our duty to support the press financially, buy the books, sponsor readings and make donations, so that those important Black writers whose voices would be silenced will continue to have a home. And we must encourage and support the new voices, the next generation of poets and writers who will fearlessly speak from and to Black people so those who want to know can hear the truth.

# Black Poet as Healer: Aneb Kgositstile's *Medicine*

It has never been enough for our poets to simply create volumes of introspection disconnected from the collective experience of the Black sojourn in the centuries since the world was ordered by the destruction white Euro-American priorities wrought. Our best poets have given their best to us because they understood our need for them to function as a type of seer, someone who could look into the soul of a moment with its sweet and bitter seconds, and dig out evidence of our humanity. Black people have needed our poets for us, not for the world, for us. We have always known the world could benefit if they listened, if they could hear. But that is not our primary concern. Our poets and our poems are for us because they restore our sight and sew up lacerations in our hearts. They scream loudly against the violence done to us and laugh even louder at the way we bend the world around us into the African inspired shapes and colors of our residual recollection.

Our best poets are for us because they speak directly to us and from the deepest folds of our memory and aspirations. Aloud their poems are familiar sounds found vibrating in the throat, that space between the belly and the mouth. The poems are polyrhythms and chords that change constantly between Monday and Sunday. They are dynamic dances celebrating pelvic centered expressions and subtle gestures made with minimum motion but maximum meaning. On the page the codes in their language pass on secrets for us, secrets shaped in our ancient history and long struggle for liberation. It may seem an unfair burden to some, but even in the 21st century Black poets are needed to pass on battle strategies to new generations and to be grounded in the healing arts ready with the salve so we can survive the wounds of a war with victories but seemingly without end. The best Black poets know that the world needs a healing and that Black people need a healing because of this world. They understand the foundation of healing is a willingness to lay your hands on someone and a commitment to give them the medicine they need.

Aneb Kgositsile is one of our best poets. She is a healer who has organized a cupboard full of secrets gathered from gardens, recipes sewn into quilts and methodology passed on in whispers. She has written them down in her new collection of poems, Medicine. This book, her fourth collection of poetry, could only come from a poet who is so planted in the Black soil and the red clay that the images she spills out over the page causes us to stop, not pause, but stop, close our eyes and let the memory drift up and into our senses were we can taste and smell and feel. Surrender to her spell is strange and wonderful because the individual memory is summoned but seems incidental. The appeal is for wide, deep connection to spirit, collective consciousness, and remembrances from so far back the names of the original tellers are difficult to recall. Medicine is a book to be carried in a pocket close to the heart. It is collective stories smuggled from person to person, family to family, community to community, south to north, north to west, across rivers and oceans. From the first lines of the title poem of this remarkable book we are forced to begin the healing:

> Comfrey leaves on the forehead for a fever;
> asphidity in a muslin pouch around the neck
> against colds and pneumonia, pungent
> odor infusing a tattered undershirt
> with a mustard-colored aura.
> It was the smell of grandmother's
> protection
> through the Winter chill.
> Medicine for thin limbs, medicine for spirit.

Reading those first lines forced me grapple with the immediate emotional response. I paused to gather myself. "...the smell of grandmother's protection/through the Winter chill/Medicine for thin limbs, medicine for spirit." It was obvious that barging into these poems wouldn't work. I had to find a way into this world of healing and past my own loss because the memory of my grandmothers had rushed furiously into my eyes and spilled over onto my face. It took a few minutes to understand that this poet Aneb Kgositsile had laid hands on me and this was a beginning, a process of restoration and strengthening and she had come to heal me and us. Accepting her gifts was the only way to have the freedom to proceed without fear, to submerge myself and allow the current take me where I needed to go.

Organized into three sections, "Ancestors' Whisper" "Praisesongs and Remembrances" and "Mission" Medicine is collection of 33 poems that reaches back and hurls us forward. Each section stands alone, yet flows seamlessly into each other. If read in sequence there is a sense that you are climbing, moving forward and upward, pausing occasionally to lookout over the emotional landscape, seeing a new sunset or feeling the wind on your skin. If read in sequence twice, the experience shifts from sequential to circular. The poems flow like life, no beginning, no end. That discovery led me to read a third and fourth time starting at various points in the collection and the results were the same. Connection to something so much greater than expected. The flow, endless and always. Her poems confirmation of the underlying belief she was taught in family and Black institutions, on Lowndes County porches and in Detroit communities. Fight for humanity from love, fight for love, endless and always.

It is evident that Aneb Kgositsile writes from the same commitment of her contemporaries, the Black Arts Movement poets who came of age as activists in the crucible of the civil rights and Black power era and reimagined the life and language of Africa's descendants while on the front lines of the battles for human rights. Like Sonia Sanchez, Haki Madhubuti, Amiri Baraka, Ntozake Shange and others, her poetic style and content is informed by her commitment to Black people and her experience fighting for Black self-determination and a humane world. She is a spiritual daughter of both Martin Luther King and Malcolm X and ancestral granddaughter of Ida B. Wells and Queen Nzinga. She writes as a daughter and a mother and a grandmother. She fashions a healing that seems only possible from woman who holds the great hope of her people while carrying the greatest pains of their travels.

Aneb Kgositsile is a poet and a scholar, an activist and a teacher. The weight of this collection is impossible without a life of study and practice, research and serious reflection, informed contemplation and unlimited imagination. With each poem we are reminded of the expectation she inherited and extends from Margaret Walker and Gwendolyn Brooks, Naomi Long Madgett and Dudley Randall. She upholds their high standards with her facility for lyrical language that sings, a historian's knowledge, skilled use of form and a vision of freedom. She honors their artistic legacy with a voice that is distinctly hers as they would want.

As one of our best poets, Aneb Kgositsile's poems are declarations of life, of Black life with no beginning or ending. Her poems are given selflessly to heal the wounds inflicted on us and to restore us and the rest of humanity to health. This book is poetry as medicine and she is the Black poet as healer strengthening us from the beginning poem to the last poem, from the first word to the very last word:

*We must keep on choosing to root ourselves in the soil of that legacy*
*that cannot be ripped out of us, a memory*
*of how to stand in the earth of our humanity,*
*to hold our footing in the ground of Love that sustains everything,*
*and stand like a tree planted by the water,*
*like Detroiters of old,*
*like the people of a city planted by the water.*
*We shall not be moved.*
*We will stand.*
*We will stand.*
*We will stand.*

*Published in 2017 as the Foreword to Medicine poetry by Aneb Kgostisile (Gloria House)*
*Broadside-Lotus Press and the University of Detroit Press.*

# A Reminder from Duke Ellington

Reached in my pocket this morning, pulled out a shiny new quarter, and the great Duke Ellington was on the back representing Washington DC Reminded me of the beauty we must create and the dignity we must maintain in the midst of hatred and violence.

Not one other person I know has found one of those quarters. On a visit to DC, I gave it to the son of my friend, the scholar Clarence Lusane. His son's name is Ellington and at 10 years old he's already an accomplished musician.

Since that first find, I've been searching for Duke on the back of quarters. I'm still looking.

# Visiting Ron Milner
May 29 1938 – July 9 2004

A few weeks before he died, I talked to the playwright Ron Milner on the phone letting him know I'd be in Detroit and would come visit. He lived in the same building as my mother and I usually visited him whenever I went to see her. That last call was a little tense because I was angry with him. He was dying, had been sick and kept the severity of it to himself. He was my brother, my mentor and friend. I was wounded, slowly bleeding emotionally knowing the inevitable was coming toward him and us.

Ron Milner was an artist with great talent, sensitivity, skill and commitment to Black art and culture. He was a poet who started out writing fiction with the intention to be a novelist, until he realized the poetry in his writing needed to flow from the mouths of the characters in his head. He became a playwright whose work was widely produced. He was a son of Detroit, the city he loved and where he always returned to write. He was a key figure in the Black Arts Movement and in that tradition, even when his plays were being produced on Broadway, Ron still produced and presented his plays in local schools, recreation centers and even on the streets of Detroit. He traveled all over the world but came back to his city and spent time talking to students of all levels and mentored a generation of writers, and theater artists. With his friend Woodie King Jr., he co-founded Detroit's Concept East Theater.

Like thousands of Black artistic youth, I was deeply inspired and motivated by the Black Arts Movement, especially the poetry that was smoking on the page and fire in performance. The BAM plays drew us because they were full of people we knew, conflict we lived and the demands we carried. The language was familiar and unapologetic. The music and movement carried us forward almost flying to ourselves and to the future the Black revolution was fashioning. Ron Milner was Detroit's standard for Black revolutionary creative writing.

In 1970 I was 16, had written dozens of poems and was beginning to perform publicly. I was reading everything from the Black Liberation Movement and spent countless hours in Vaughn's bookstore where its founder Ed Vaughn would direct me to various books and hold lengthy discussions on African and African American history. That store is where I could get copies of the many journals of Black revolutionary art and thought like Soul Book and the Journal of Black Poetry, Black World and the Black Scholar. It was also the first place I'd go to find the new published poetry of the Black Arts poets like Imamu Amiri Baraka, Sonia Sanchez, Haki Madhubuti (then Don L. Lee). The more I immersed myself in the writing of the Black Arts Movement the more determined I was to be a writer in that tradition. I was a precocious revolutionary teenager and certain I was a badass poet.

I assembled my first manuscript of about 20 poems and called Ron to ask him if he'd read them. I was prepared to mail them but he told me to come the next day to the theater where he was in rehearsal. Arriving at the designated time and waiting for about an hour until the rehearsal took a break, I studied Ron directing. He finally came over, took me into a room with a large table and told me, "Go sit down there at the end." Of course I complied, while he sat at the other end with my manuscript. He read a poem, than another and another. Sometimes he'd mutter an unintelligible comment or say "uh-huh, uh-huh." Finally, he closed the folder, looked at me for a second and said, "Is this it?"

I was stunned and momentarily speechless giving him reason to repeat, "Is this it?" "Those are my best poems." He looked at me again and said, "It's not good enough." I was devastated and he could see it. I wanted his approval and wanted my poems to be worthy of the Black Arts Movement.

Ron Milner, a writer I revered, then went on to say, "You obviously have talent and something you want to say, but you're not ready yet. To be a writer it has to become a practice, you have to write all the time. You have to learn how to write so people want to read or hear or experience what you are saying to them. It takes commitment and discipline. We'll see if you're serious. I hope you are."

I remember that conversation as if it happened today. From the day he read my bad poetry until right before he died, I sent Ron my work for his critique, his honest and sometime painful critique of my work. He always made time and always made my work better.

I went to visit him in Detroit. He was clearly ill but didn't want to discuss it, dismissing my inquiries with, "I wish people would stop trying to make a big deal about this."

We spent the next two hours watching the Detroit Pistons, listening to John Coltrane and talking about writing. I reminded him that he almost destroyed my desire to be a writer. We laughed about it for a long time. It was the last time I saw my friend, mentor and brother. He died a few weeks later. I think about him often, visiting him in my memories and in his plays which I read periodically as a reminder of what a Black revolutionary creative writer is supposed to do.

# Liner Notes – Cassandra Wilson *Belly of the Sun* (2002)

The first time I met Cassandra Wilson we were both performing along with other artists in a little juke joint in Laurel, Mississippi in support of a group of African American women poultry workers who were on strike. That was more than 20 years ago and even then, in that small, dark, crowded, smoke-filled place smelling of fried chicken, catfish and alcohol, even then and there it was clear that Cassandra was a special artist. Playing her guitar and singing with a band of women musicians, she had already started experimenting with the setting for her voice. That night she was accompanied by a bass plyer, a percussionist and Rhonda Richmond on violin. (Rhonda plays piano on this album and wrote the song "Road So Clear"). Her voice was set in sparse rhythmic arrangements sweetened by the haunting tones of the violin. Imagine a rural juke joint, late at night, people getting juiced and the smell of lust draped on everything, yet everyone stopped and listened, leaned into hear ever note and let her take them deeper into the space they were trying to get to.

It was an amazing thing to witness. As our friendship grew over the next few years, I came to understand the power of that night for her. She was home, in Mississippi, singing with and for her people, reaching inside of them, herself and history, trying to see the future, hoping she would represent their dreams and explode any boundaries that blocked them. When she decided to return home to record this album, it wasn't a surprise. It was time.

Her initial concept was to go to the Mississippi Delta and do a blues-based record. This is a natural, almost instinctive starting point for her. The blues is the door to the deeper chambers of American music where Cassandra often wanders around in search of clues and answers. Even though she had an idea it was just a sketch, a seed that would become some of what was envisioned at the beginning. She has always approached her work without detailed plans so she is open to what the process brings.

As is usually the case with her, she first sets out to create an environment for the music to unfold. She began by looking for a place that would put her close to the spirit she was searching for. With help from several Mississippi friends, she traveled through the Delta looking for the right space, finally settling on what used to the old train station in Clarksdale. Over two days the train station was transformed into a recording studio. Calling on the extraordinarily talented members of her touring band (Marvin Sewell, Kevin Breit, Jeff Haynes, Cyro Baptista and Mark Peterson) as the foundation, Cassandra set out as both producer and performer to record the album she titled *Belly of the Sun*.

Under difficult conditions, including a scorching August heat, and working with her long-time engineer, Danny Kopleson, and a half dozen supporting staff, over the next ten days Cassandra recorded 15 songs (two of them Hot Tamales and You Gotta Move in an old boxcar after being kicked out of the train station for a wedding reception that had previously scheduled there.) In addition to her band, she enlisted the talents of several Mississippi musicians, including Boogaloo Ames, who, in his 80 plus years, walked slowly to the piano and sat down where you could see the years fall away when he started playing (*Darkness on the Delta* and *Rock Me Baby*). From her hometown Jackson Mississippi, she brought in Jesse Robinson (Show Me a Love), a guitarist who had performed often with her father, Herman Fowlkes; singers Jewell Bass, Vasti Jackson, Patrice Moncell and Henry Rhodes (Only a Dream in Rio); the gifted young drummer Xavyon (X) on several songs.

What began as a blues-based record became an experience in creative discovery. The sessions in Mississippi explored Blues, Jazz, African, Brazilian, Pop and R+B. It ventured into social issues and spiritual life, love and lust, the contemplative and the common. By the time Cassandra returned to New York, there was a clearer picture of what this record would be. But it wasn't finished. She had been approached about doing something with the young, soulful singer India.Arie who has listed Cassandra as one of her influences. It just so happened that Cassandra had written a song that she wanted to do with another singer and India was perfect for it. In a

New York studio she recorded *Just Another Parade*, the Bob Dylan song *Shelter from the Storm* and brought in children from New York's M>S> 44 to add their young, hopeful energy to Waters of March. And then it was finished.

This album has the classic feel of a Cassandra Wilson journey where borders and boundaries are sometimes pushed, sometimes expanded, sometimes eliminated but always discounted as limitations. It is the full power of her Mississippi roots and the roots of American music. On this album Cassandra reaches beyond musical and national boundaries to say something about who we all are and why we must listen to each other. On this album that amazing voice of hers tells us more distinctly than ever that if we listen to each other, we will hear the thing that connects us, the sound of us breathing and loving and trying to understand why borders and boundaries are not limitations.

# Haiku for Sonia Sanchez

Blues lyrics at dawn
Poetry hums the night mood
Flowers from her song

# Full Moon of Sonia

Sonia Sanchez is a poet a Black woman poet a Black Arts Movement poet a world poet a teacher poet a warrior poet from the warrior generation. I have no idea when we met decades ago, it is as if our lives were always connected. She has inspired and taught me, corrected and supported me through the struggles of our people and my struggles in life. She is the one who goes to sit at the bedside of our dying elders, playing music and reading to them as they transition. She gives her number to anyone who wants to call her, even when I've advised her against it. With an unassailable love for Black people, she stands for the sisters, the humanity and centrality of women and girls and loves us brothers so hard and so evident that it helps us to stand too, even when all the false narrative but heavy weight of Black manhood is a barrier to our understanding and growth.

***

Sonia Sanchez always showed up when I called for me and for us. A running joke between us, which she occasionally shares with her audience, is that whenever I used to call it was to ask her to come to some dangerous conflict with the KKK or other violent racists. She never hesitated, saw it as her duty and trusted we would protect her, which we always did mostly in ways she couldn't even see and still doesn't know. We called her because we needed the magic of Sonia Sanchez, a poet, marching down the streets of New York or the back roads of Georgia, armed with poems soaked with all our beauty and power and mightier than the lies of white supremacy and male supremacy, to steel us for the fight we knew we were in and the ones to come.

***

In 2004, I co-produced with Thomas Jones III "Full Moon of Sonia" an 18 song studio album of Sonia Sanchez reading selections from her poems with music. We recorded it in Atlanta with some of our best musicians and some from other cities. Sonia's magic made it a creative event that brought dozens of poets, actors, musicians, educators and activists into the studio to be a witness and participant in this project. We worked night and day with limited budget and a lot of volunteer help. In a two week period we recorded 26 songs and mixed and mastered 18 for the album. Tom directed, I produced and Patdro Harris choreographed the live performance of this work for the National Black Arts Festival. Diana Stevens of VIA Productions handled all the business and kept us running. From the poems on the page to completing the recording and the live performance it was one of my favorite creative experiences because of Sonia's magic.

# A Tribute to Amiri Baraka
October 7, 1934 – January 9, 2014

Amiri Baraka's death on January 9, 2014, caused the Black ecosystem of institutions, intellectuals, artists and activists committed to our century's long fight for human rights to stagger under the weight of the loss and its possible meanings. Even as we gathered ourselves to publicly mourn and honor him, to write and read our thoughts and feelings, there was a sense that a significant change had occurred in our world of resistance and struggle. In the weeks after his death, when we had not quite found our footing, our brother–Jackson, Mississippi Mayor Chokwe Lumumba–transitioned suddenly, followed by one of our great historians Vincent Harding, our beautiful storyteller Maya Angelou and the relentless advocate for African people Elombe Brath. It was as if Baraka's death was not enough to force us to see we are reaching the end of the era of the Warrior Generation.

Imamu Amiri Baraka was many things to our people, we collectively and us individually. He was an artist with exceptionally deep perception and talent, an educator, a political and spiritual leader, a revolutionary strategist and institution builder, a fearless warrior against all who would diminish Black people, an insightful teacher, a scholar of African American history and culture, a determined advocate for Black self-determination, a husband and father, and a prolific writer who created a significant body of work that included poetry, plays, essays, fiction, music and scholarly articles. The many forms in which he came to us were the result of his never ending quest to find a way to give everything he had in service of the people he loved, Black people and humanity. Even his names reminded us of his changes: LeRoi Jones, Ameer Baraka, Imamu Baraka, and Amiri Baraka. We were inspired and sometimes confused by his shape shifting. Sometimes we were angered by it and in opposition to it. But we never doubted it was him. We were never unsure of his voice or that he was our warrior, that all of his prodigious gifts were focused on and fueled by our demand for self-determination and justice.

Amiri Baraka was one of many intellectuals of his generation whose scholarly research and study, writing, teaching and work actually influenced the political struggle of African Americans and called countless young artists, activists and scholars to work on behalf of our people. But Baraka's political influence is extraordinary in his generation of exceptional thinkers and workers because of his direct involvement and leadership of significant historical events in the Black Liberation Movement. That leadership grew from an underlying principle that remained consistent in his activism. Baraka's work has always been based on building institutions that would engage greater numbers of people in an organized effort to advance the struggle. Some of these institutions were local, community-based organizations and some also had national and international scope and impact. He believed that where ever we are it is necessary to build, strengthen or expand structures that will help us wage and sustain our efforts.

Throughout his public life he founded or co-founded newspapers, theatre companies, cultural centers, community organizations, national liberation organizations and numerous coalitions and united fronts. While he is widely acknowledged as the most influential artist of the Black Arts Movement, for the past 50 years he also built cultural institutions including The Black Arts Repertory Theatre, Spirit House, Kimako's Blues People and Blue Ark as platforms to nurture, engage and organize actors, writers, directors, poets, musicians and cultural workers. The political formations he co-founded and played significant leadership roles in included the Committee for Unified Newark, Congress of African People, National Black Political Convention, National Black Assembly, African Liberation Support Committee and many others. He also formed and supported several publications including Black NewArk, Unity and Struggle and Black Nation Magazine. In the days preceding his death Baraka was still organizing, supporting and building another political formation, the mayoral campaign of his son, Ras Baraka. Ras won the election and is now the Mayor of Newark 44 years after his father organized the first Black Nationalist led electoral movement in a major city that succeeded in electing Newark's first Black mayor Ken Gibson.

Amiri Baraka left more than forty published works as a record of his research, thought, and constantly developing consciousness. It is evidence of his dedication and seemingly boundless capacity for productivity. It is also evidence of his understanding that we, the writers and artists, the intellectual warriors, the scholars and teachers, have a sacred, crucial role in our people's history and future. There are many pages of his writings that have never been published and hopefully will begin to make their way to us in the near future so we may further benefit from his thought and work and a life of struggle that is worthy of the ancestors who inspired him to give his life and gifts to us.

"When I die, the consciousness I carry I will to Black people."– Amiri Baraka.

*Originally Published in the Black Scholar September 17, 2014.*

# Maya Angelou – Art from Her People, Art for the World

    Maya Angelou's transition to one of our ancestors today leaves us again with a profound sense of loss and also another critical moment to reflect. The loss is monumental because she was a giant amongst the public figures that have impacted art, culture and politics for the past 60 years. The moment to reflect is important because we must not think only about what she gave us but also what she should expect from us.

    Dr. Angelou was a multi-discipline artist who created as a writer, singer, composer, dancer, actress, poet, director. Her best known works were her popular poetry and the stunning memoirs filled with the beauty of African American life and the terror of violence against girls and women and racist violence against her community. She spoke with honesty and empathy that revealed a deep spiritual quality that became known worldwide as the voice of someone who believed in the good of humanity and the necessary work of human beings to allow that good to be revealed. She was an artist of conscience who spoke often and eloquently through her art and speeches against injustice, violence and oppression. The potency of her art, the reason it resonates so powerfully is because she developed her incredible talent to the highest level of skill and craft but most importantly because of the depth of the content. Her work came from digging way down into the language and customs, the food and the dance, the music and the nuances of Black life. She was a highly educated woman who never stopped learning and who understood that her mission, her sacred mission was to serve her people with the great gifts she was given and the knowledge she acquired.

    Maya Angelou was an early advocate for the unity and liberation of Africa and the Diaspora. She promoted African and African American culture, holding it up as an equal to the cultures of the world. Mother Maya, walked this earth like a queen, regal and adorned with the self confidence that comes from knowing you are a descendant of people who could not be defeated. Her poems and stories, her speeches and conversations were soaked in that knowledge. She knew that even if it took 500 years or 1000 years, we will be a free people. She also understood that complacency and self-hatred don't lead to acts of resistance and courage. Faith and love, self-love and the undying believe in our humanity were the lessons she taught us. She spoke to us as a divine voice, reminding us, pushing us, pulling us to love ourselves and others. You cannot experience her art and life without feeling that divine voice, rich and full of laughter, scolding us when necessary, challenging us always to be the better us, the higher us, the great us.

Too often with our revered sheroes and heroes we allow them to be airbrushed into pretty icons of irrelevancy. We fall into worshiping the polished image, the part that shines in public, the awards and accolades that get pasted on school posters. But Maya Angelou must be remembered as a champion of our right to be full human beings. Like other artists of her generation, she took great risks to stand with our people and oppressed people everywhere in the fight for justice. She was a friend, supporter and contemporary of both Malcolm X and Martin Luther King. She stood on picket lines and raised money for human rights causes. Her weapon of choice was the truth and she wielded it in poems and books, plays and music, education and a relentless demand that we be treated as human beings and that all human beings rise up and defeat the forces of violence and racism, sexism and oppression, war and poverty. And while her favored weapons were artistic, she was also willing to put on some marching shoes. And now, while we grapple with our sorrow and the fact that we must face the world without her steady guidance, we have to also face ourselves and ask if we are willing to speak the truth, to take the risk, to stand with courage like hers and transform this world.

*Originally published on blackartinamerica.com*

# Rockin' with Jimi Hendrix

As a teenager I was a Black power activist writing poetry, organizing students, devouring African American literature and listening to all kinds of music but mostly Jazz, Soul and select rock and roll, especially a left-handed guitarist from Seattle.

On May 2, 1969 Jimi Hendrix played his second and final concert in Detroit and with two carloads of students I headed downtown to see him at Cobo Hall. My friend Geoffrey Grier and I were two Black radical teens who had mastered the art of getting into concerts free because we were usually broke. The plan was to use our great skills to get in to see Hendrix. Geoff was so confident in our abilities that he promised the other people with us that he would also secure their entry and directed them to a side door of Cobo Hall to wait until we opened it from the inside.

For the next 30 minutes, the two of us walked completely around the massive arena, tried every door and talked to everyone who looked like they worked there in an attempt to get in. We were spectacularly unsuccessful and wound up on an upper walk way, leaning on a rail looking out on the Detroit River, discussing our failure before we returned to our patiently waiting friends and confessed defeat. As we stood there, with Canada looking back at us, three limousines pulled up below us. We watched the doors fly open and some white men and women got out and then a man threw his legs out the door, hesitated a moment and finally unfolded his body from the back seat. Standing one flight below us was Jimi Hendrix and nine or ten others including his band. Without saying a word to each other, Geoff and I hit the stairs with great speed and stealth and made our way down just as the group begin to walk single-file through the door. We fell in behind them and walked right into Cobo Hall following Jimi Hendrix and entourage into a large green room with food and liquor, soft drinks and big couches where we planted ourselves as someone passed us a joint. Hendrix left for a moment and when he came back sat on a coach directly across the room from us.

There was some banter about the tour. They joked and teased, laughed, smoked marijuana and cigarettes and drank whiskey and rum. The opening act was on-stage and the faint sound of their music drifted in. After about fifteen minutes I noticed Hendrix staring at us with a look of puzzlement. His gaze was fixed long enough for others to notice because it got quiet and the entire room focused on us. Finally he said, "I bet you two cats don't have tickets to the show." We smiled but didn't speak. He kept staring and then started laughing and so did everyone in the room. He asked us how we did it and kept laughing as we told the story. Someone came in and said, "Jimi we have to get ready to go on." With cigarette in hand, Hendrix stood up walked to the door where he stopped and told Noel Redding the bassist in the Jimi Hendrix Experience, "How about getting my young friends some seats." He turned to us and said, "Thanks so much for loving my music." And then he was gone.

Redding took us out into the arena and sat us on the stage in the wings but where we could be seen. Geoffrey saw a friend who was ushering that night and asked him to open the door for a couple of our people who didn't have tickets and were waiting outside. When the lights dimmed he opened the door and our friends were still there with about 200 other people who rushed in just as Jimi Hendrix hit the first cord and Cobo Arena erupted with the sound of the bluesman who'd become the most influential guitarist of his generation. Some would say to this day. For a minute we were widely celebrated and admired by our friends who wanted to hear the story over and over. After high school Geoffrey and I lost touch for a while. I'd heard that he and his brother David Allan Grier both moved to California to be closer to their father William H. Grier, the noted Black psychiatrist and co-author of Black Rage an important book of the Black Power era. A lot of life had been lived when we reconnect, and when we did, the night we met Jimi Hendrix was a memory, a story we told and continue to tell to anyone who will listen.

# Danny Glover at the Black Rodeo

In 1986, I saw Danny Glover at the Bill Pickett Rodeo in Atlanta. Coming off of his role in the western film Silverado, he rode his horse skillfully into the arena with a group of Black professional cowboys and cowgirls. They lined up for the playing of the national anthems, Star Spangled and Lift Every Voice and Sing as was a tradition in Black institutions throughout the 20th century. When the Star Spangled was played Danny sat on his horse quietly, did not take off his hat or put his hand over his heart. When the Black National Anthem was played he did both and sang and seemed to also sit higher in the saddle, the power and pride of generations of African Americans radiating through his posture and presentation. It was a time before we had the capacity to record everything and post it on social media. There was a time, when every major event in the Black community included the singing of the Black National Anthem. It connected us to each other and the past. It gave us faith in our future and our people. I was a Black History Month speaker at an Atlanta middle school recently and the staff handed out the lyrics to students and teachers because they didn't know the lyrics. I thought back to that moment at the rodeo and wished those students understood what it meant for us to know the power of the Black nation that gave birth to them and the foundations and traditions they stand on.

*Lift every voice and sing*
*Till earth and heaven ring*
*Ring with the harmonies of Liberty*
*Let our rejoicing rise*
*High as the list'ning skies*
*Let it resound loud as the rolling sea*
*Sing a song full of the faith that the dark past has taught us*
*Sing a song full of the hope that the present has brought us*
*Facing the rising sun of our new day begun*
*Let us march on till victory is won*[2]

James Weldon Johnson 1899

# Celebrating Billie Holiday: Cassandra Wilson Salutes the Jazz Icon with New Album

April 7, marks the 100th anniversary of the birth of Billie Holiday, born Eleanora Fagan. It is also the day that Cassandra Wilson releases the much-anticipated CD Coming Forth by Day, her extraordinary homage to Billie Holiday. There have been and will be many tributes to Holiday, some of them exceptional. But it is Wilson more than any of the other great vocalists of this time, who is clearly the musical and spiritual granddaughter of Lady Day. Granddaughter because her most direct influence was the late Abby Lincoln who was also deeply affected musically by Holiday. That musical lineage, Holiday, Lincoln, is undeniable in this new album.

*Coming Forth by Day* is Grammy Award-winning jazz singer Cassandra Wilson with all of her gifts and experience fully engaged and on display. On this album it is her singular voice, the ability to read a lyric in a way not heard before, and her encyclopedic musical vocabulary working at its highest level to discover something new. She is not trying to imitate Lady Day. Wilson's intention is clearly to dig deeper and say something significant about Holiday and how who she was and who she'd come from was always present in her music.

Consistent with the jazz musicians of her era, Holiday had an exceptionally productive career that included more than 300 recorded songs. Implicit in Billie Holiday's music is a demand for recognition that her unique storytelling emerged from the experience of Black people living under de jure and de facto segregation and oppression. Holiday understood and found beauty in that experience because she knew it was capable of facing its sorrow and strength, its joy and hurt, which she could often project in the same phrase. It was evident in the way she attacked and presented a story. Her songs were public and private conversations with her unmistakable statement of certainty and the required space for an emotional response from the listener. Holiday never hovered on the surface of a lyric and never relied on the pure unique sound of her voice. She was always deep inside it, seeking its secrets. She also demanded recognition of her truth explicitly. In the context and subtext of her songs is the struggle as woman to live, love, work and to laugh, play, cry, to fall and to stand, to be fully human. Her power as an artist was never felt more than when she performed the emotionally wrenching "Strange Fruit" as protest against the lynching of Black people which seemed an acceptable practice of American culture of the time.

Cassandra Wilson has also created an impressive body of work that includes 20 solo albums and dozens of collaborations with a wide-range of artists from Wynton Marsalis to the Roots. She too she is known for digging deep inside a lyric and finding something undiscovered or under said. Her own artistic practice has been built on finding and deciphering the coded meaning, the nuances and subtleties of a song as if they were symbols woven in the panels of a quilt. Like Billie Holiday, there is an implicit demand in her music too, be it for love or to be heard, to dance or worship or for us to become better human beings. The explicit demand is also there. When Wilson sings "Strange Fruit," it is not just protest, she is saying it is unacceptable to have to revisit those lyrics today when they were first performed by Holiday in 1939.

The title Coming Forth by Day is from ancient Kemetic (Egyptian) text regarding life, death and after-life and served as a source for contemplation. The two-year long process of creating this album was both musical and spiritual and began in earnest with Wilson's deepened understanding that Holiday's message still resonates. Wilson discovered the often obscured power of Holiday's life and the triumphant quality of her musical legacy as evidence of a journey of purpose, empowerment and enduring victory instead of the usual depiction of her as tragic victim.

As we remember and celebrate the great talent and contribution of Billie Holiday, we have the good fortune to also anticipate the constant surprises that Cassandra Wilson shares with us. Coming Forth by Day is full of surprises and is one of Wilson's most remarkable recordings in a career filled with remarkable recordings.

*Originally Published in Rolling Out Magazine April 7 2015*

# Prince: Art as Spiritual Practice

Prince will be remembered for his genius and the sustained and extremely productive artistic output as a virtuoso musician, songwriter and producer for the past four decades. He was such a prolific creative force that music seemed to pour out of him effortlessly. The quality of his work is proof that it did not. The musical legacy Prince gave us is the work of a disciplined, committed artist who worked at his art relentlessly, studied music and other forms constantly, explored and contemplated technology and the humanities. In the quiet of his internal spaces with the lovely noise of ideas clamoring for attention and development, he could focus as all great artists do and transform the ideas into art, pulling them one by one out of his head into the world where he shaped them into the sound that was uniquely his. Above his celebrity, the persona and mystique, he was a practicing artist who loved the language of music, the musicians who speak that language and the people who can hear it.

He also understood the transformational importance and power of art and used it frequently as a tool, a weapon in the fight for a just and humane society. He challenged bigotry and racism through his music and the visual language he created to extend his ideas. Prince forced us to look at and accept our beautiful difference through his own costuming and theatrics while always performing with bands more representative of society than everyone else. Black, Hispanic and white, female and male, old and young, lesbian, gay and straight all found a place on stage with him when no one else had the understanding or courage.

His extraordinary contribution also included an ability to hear the whispers between musical genres and to facilitate their public conversation by expanding the vocabulary of contemporary American music deeply steeped in African American musical traditions of blues, jazz, soul, funk, gospel and rock. Consistent with the text and subtext often heard in those forms, Prince played between the secularity of human behavior and the sacredness of human yearning. His exploration of the carnal desires of sexuality and sexual identity was always balanced by attention he paid to the importance of love. Prince songs speak openly of love that is intimate and reckless, romantic and committed and familial for those close and all of humankind we've yet to meet.

Inside his deep body of work Prince placed a persistent invitation. He was on a quest for deeper spiritual understanding and connection and he always invited us to travel with him beyond the obvious to something more profound. He wanted us to see that in the fabric of his and the stitching of his music was a map to a spiritual journey where dancing was heavily encouraged. Whether we consciously understood or not, engaging in his recorded or live music took us there and that is the reason it moved us so. He was like the rest of us, searching for deeper meaning in human life and its relationship to everything else. Like John Coltrane perfecting his musicianship so he could get closer to God and better serve God's people, Prince understood his great gifts meant something beyond entertaining. He dedicated himself to the exploration of music, the elevation of his own abilities and a life of creating remarkable work. He lived what the poet Sonia Sanchez calls, "Art as spiritual practice."

*Originally published in Rolling Out Magazine April 23 201??*

# When Lupita Nyong'o Won the Oscar

A barrage of Black shame poured out on social media when Lupita Nyong'o won the Oscar for her performance in 12 Years a Slave. Much of it carried the usual comments about why white people would give an Oscar to a Black woman for portraying a slave but not for other roles. We don't like it. We don't want to see it. It makes us uncomfortable yet, Black people saw and applauded Tarentino's cartoon version of slavery, Django. Perhaps because it was cartoonish and devoid of the violence visited upon Black people for generations. Maybe the lack of the torture and rape, the starvation and deprivation in the cartoon slavery lets us disassociate from the ancestors who endured that terror.

There seems to be a misconception about what Lupita Nyong'o achieved. While it appeared she played a slave, what she did in her performance was beautiful. She invoked and portrayed an ancestor who like millions of others survived the horrors of slavery with their incredible strength and dignity so we could be here today. They should be remembered and praised and so should she for insuring their presence on screen reminded us of the beauty and power of the people we came from.

# An Answer

We are fighting for our humanity, to be whole, to be who we are in concert with the rest of humanity without the necessity to yield the parts of us that others find offensive because of the narratives created to diminish us and justify our exploitation.

# Ain't Gonna Let Nobody Turn Us 'Round

when the shadows chased us
all the way home
and the force of their
intentions broke the windows
of our mother's house
we looked for stones
to arm our slingshots
and the songs came flying to
us like birds with jet engines
wings spread wide
history spilling its colors across an ocean
and the only thing we knew for sure
were the poems we painted and left
like footprints in the mountains

ahhhhh yessss
the poems
with melody and harmony
rhythm and history
the poems
more than the text so textured
it could be woven into a fine garment
hung across weary shoulders
like a choir robe rising with outstretched hands

yes
the poems
sitting under a fedora
growing like trees
on a tongue moving

nature
rising and falling
like dancers caressing
the notes that infect
their bodies when the lights disappear

the poems
the weight of their truth splashing
around in blood
slipping on placenta
the dirty poems
full of shit and surprise

we want the truth

and when the shadows chase us
all the way home
and the force of their
intentions tries to break the windows
of our mother's house
we still find stones
arm our slingshots
sing new songs so the birds will
fly to us like rockets
wings spread wide
spilling our colors across the planet
we know for sure
we will always paint our poems and leave them
like footprints in the mountains

no more slavery
no more slavery
no more slavery
over me

*Originally published in Africology: the Journal of Pan-African Studies, Vol. 4(2). 2010.*

# Notes

[1]Cesaire, Aime. 1975. Notes on a Return to the Native Land in *The Negritude Poets*. New York: Viking Press.

[2]Douglass, Frederick. 2016. The Meaning of July Fourth to the Negro in *The Essential Douglass*. Hackett Press.

[3]Jacobs, Harriet Ann. 2008. *Incidents in the Life of a Slave Girl* in *A Will to Be Free, Vol 2*. Wilder Publications.

[4]Horne, Gerald. 2014. The Counter-Revolution of 1776. New York: NYU Press.

[5]Wells, Ida B. 1970. *Crusade for Justice: The Autobiography of Ida B. Wells*. Chicago: University of Chicago Press.

[6]Phillips, Kevin. 2014. *The Emerging Republican Majority*. New Jersey: Princeton University Press.

[7]Johnson, James Weldon. www.poetryfoundation.org/poems-and-poets/poems/detail/46549

[8]http://www.nbcnews.com/id/27738018/ns/us_news-life/t/obama-election-spurs-race threats-crimes/#.WRr042jys2w

[9]https://www.splcenter.org/fighting-hate/intelligence-report/2008/radical right%E2%80%99s-reaction-election-barack-obama

[10]https://www.loc.gov/rr/program/bib/ourdocs/DredScott.html

[11]Davis, Angela. 2016. *Freedom is a Constant Struggle*. Chicago: Haymarket Books.

[12]http://www.operationghettostorm.org

[13]Johnson, James Weldon. www.poetryfoundation.org/poems-and poets/poems/detail/46549

[14]X, Malcolm. 1965. *Malcolm X Speaks*. New York: Pathfinder Press.